Editor
Mara Ellen Guckian

Editor in Chief
Brent L. Fox, M. Ed.

Creative Director
Sarah M. Fournier

Cover Artist
Sarah Kim

Illustrator
Mark Mason

Art Coordinator
Renée Mc Elwee

Imaging
Amanda R. Harter
Crystal-Dawn Keitz

Publisher
Mary D. Smith, M.S. Ed.

For standards correlations, visit
*http://www.teachercreated.com
/standards/*.

Author

Tracy Edmunds, M.A. Ed.

Teacher Created Resources
12621 Western Avenue
Garden Grove, CA 92841
www.teachercreated.com
ISBN: 978-1-4206-8261-8
©2020 Teacher Created Resources
Reprinted, 2021
Made in U.S.A.

Table of Contents

Table of Contents (cont.)

Introduction

Science is the study of the world around us. Students experience science every day without knowing it! Learning about how the world works can be fascinating, but sometimes, students must find fun and accessible science topics *before* they realize how enjoyable science can be. The passages in this book contain high-interest topics that will immediately hook students and challenge them to see science at work in their own experiences. From learning how living things adapt to each season to exploring different types of energy, students will enjoy practicing their informational reading skills with interesting science topics.

This book is arranged into four sections:

Science Practices   **Life Science**
Earth and Space Science   **Physical Science**

Within each section are a number of five-page units, each of which explores an important science topic. Most pages feature reading passages and response questions. Some pages include science-related worksheets. Within each science discipline, the units are sequential and build upon one another.

Teachers should not feel restricted by a daily warm-up activity. Sometimes, schedules change. A morning assembly, a make-up lesson, or just an extra-busy day can easily throw off the classroom schedule for days. A teacher never knows what his or her week is going to look like. *Let's Get This Day Started: Science* units do not need to be completed every day or even every other day. Teachers can take their time and arrange the activities to fit their own schedules. A teacher may choose to do a unit a week (one passage a day), or, at other times, spread a unit out over a few weeks. There is no right or wrong way.

These pages are meant to be a supplement, not a substitute, for a science curriculum. Use them in conjunction with science lessons whenever possible.

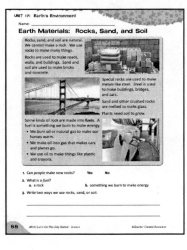

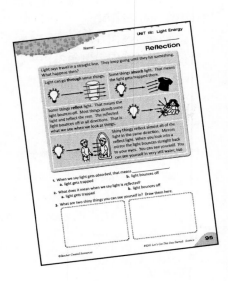

How to Use This Book

When introducing each new science topic, a teacher may choose to have the class read the passages together as a group before asking them to read each passage again on their own. A teacher may also choose to have students reread passages after a science lesson or unit to reinforce and review learning. **Note:** Some units incorporate photographs in student activities. These add a realistic element to the writing prompts and engage students by providing a real-life connection for their learning. When making photocopies of these pages, it is best to use the photo setting so the images are easier to see. You may also choose to supplement certain passages with related photographs or other visual aids you might have available.

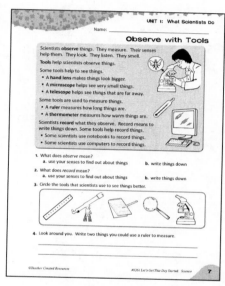

The multiple-choice questions in *Let's Get This Day Started: Science* assess all levels of comprehension—from recall to critical thinking. These questions offer an opportunity to teach students test-taking skills. If an answer choice includes an unfamiliar word, the correct answer can still be found by the process of elimination. Remind students to read every answer choice! If the answer doesn't jump out at them, they can get it right by crossing out the wrong answers first.

The missing words or phrases for fill-in-the blank questions can be found within the reading passage. These questions reinforce important scientific vocabulary and concepts.

Short written-response questions require students to connect new learning to their own experience or to apply the concepts in the passage to a new situation. These questions are intended to encourage students to "show what they know," and responses will vary based on students' reading, writing, and thinking development.

Use the *Tracking Sheet* on page 106 to keep track of which passages you have given to your students, or distribute copies of the sheet for students to monitor their own progress. An Answer Key is provided on pages 106–112.

Name: _____

What Do Scientists Do?

Scientists ask questions. They want to know how things work. They want to find out why things happen.

What questions do scientists ask?

Scientists ask questions such as these:

- Do plants need the Sun to grow?
- What kinds of animals live in this pond?
- Where do mountains come from?
- How many people can live on Earth?

How do scientists try to answer their questions?

- They **observe** things. This means they use their senses. They look with their eyes. They listen with their ears.
- They **test** things. They use tools to **measure** how big, how fast, or how hot things are.

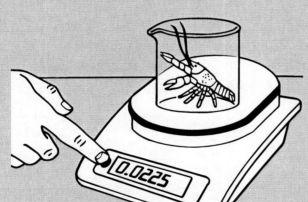

- They **write down** what they find.
- They use what they find to try to answer their questions.

Science is not a secret!

Scientists share what they find. They tell other scientists about what they found. They write about it. Other scientists can try the same tests. They want to know if others find the same things.

1. Scientists try to answer questions by _____.
   a. observing things   **b.** doing tests   **c.** both **a** and **b**

2. Scientists _____ their observations.
   a. hide   **b.** share

3. What science question would you ask?

_____

_____

Name: _____

Observe with Tools

Scientists **observe** things. They measure. Their senses help them. They look. They listen. They smell.

Tools help scientists observe things.

Some tools help to see things.

- A **hand lens** makes things look bigger.
- A **microscope** helps us see very small things.
- A **telescope** helps us see things that are far away.

Some tools are used to measure things.

- A **ruler** measures how long things are.
- A **thermometer** measures how warm things are.

Scientists **record** what they observe. *Record* means "to write things down." Some tools help record things.

- Some scientists use notebooks to record things.
- Some scientists use computers to record things.

1. What does *observe* mean?
   a. to use your senses to find out about things   **b.** to write things down

2. What does *record* mean?
   a. to use your senses to find out about things   **b.** to write things down

3. Circle the tools that scientists use to see things better.

4. Look around you. Write two things you could measure with a ruler.

_____

_____

Name: _____

Measuring Tools

Scientists ask questions. They want to know how things work. They want to find out why things happen. They **observe** things. This means that they use their senses. They look with their eyes. They listen with their ears.

Scientists use tools to measure how big, fast, or hot things are. They write down what they find.

Directions: Look at each picture, and answer the question.

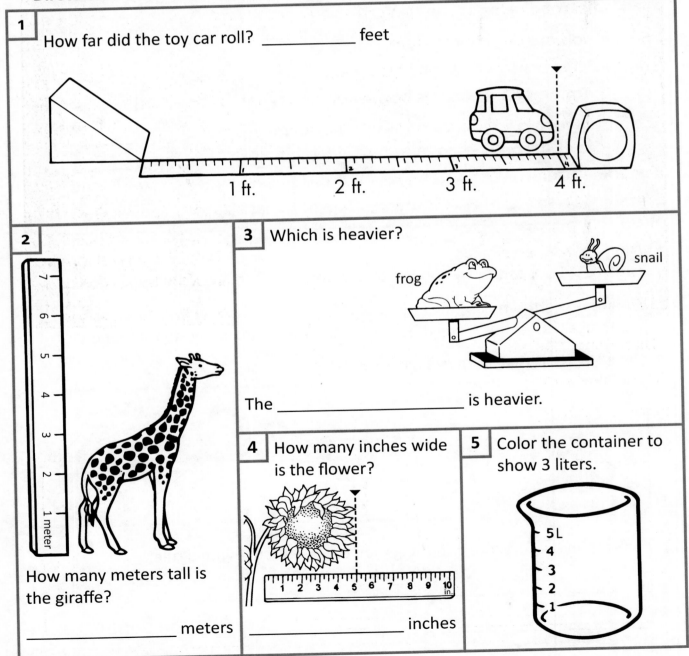

1 How far did the toy car roll? _____ feet

1 ft.   2 ft.   3 ft.   4 ft.

2 How many meters tall is the giraffe?

1 meter

_____ meters

3 Which is heavier?

frog   snail

The _____ is heavier.

4 How many inches wide is the flower?

1 2 3 4 5 6 7 8 9 10 in.

_____ inches

5 Color the container to show 3 liters.

5L
4
3
2
1

Name: _____

Scientists Compare Things

Scientists **compare** things. They look at how things are the **same**. They look at how things are **different**. Things can be different in size. Planets are very big. Germs are very small.

Things can move at different speeds. Rockets move fast. Cars move slower than rockets. But cars move faster than bikes.

Slowest ——————————————➤ **Fastest**

Scientists put things in order. Here are three animals. They are in order by size.

Smallest ——————————————➤ **Biggest**

You can put the same things in a different order. Below, they are in order by how many legs they have.

Fewest legs ——————————————➤ **Most legs**

Directions: Circle the correct word in each sentence.

1. Mountains are   *bigger*   *smaller*   than hills.

2. Rabbits move   *slower*   *faster*   than snails.

3. Think of three animals. Draw them in order from *smallest* to *biggest*. Label them.

Smallest ——————————————➤ **Biggest**

Name: _____

Cause and Effect

When scientists want to answer a question, they can look for causes and effects.

- A **cause** is a reason *why* something happened.
- The **effect** is *what* happened.

Sasha is cold. She puts on a jacket. She gets warmer.

- **Cause:** Sasha puts on a jacket.
- **Effect:** She gets warmer.

Scientists want to know what causes things.

- Why did that plant die?
- Why do we have seasons?
- What makes wind?

Here are some causes and effects:

Cause (*Why something happened*)	**Effect** (*What happened next*)
- The plant did not get water. →	The plant died.
- Earth spins. →	We have day and night.
- She hit the drum. →	It made a loud sound.

Directions: Fill in the missing *causes* or *effects*. You can use your imagination as long as your answer makes sense.

Cause		Effect
1. _____ _____	→	**The balloon flew away.**
2. **I practiced my spelling words.**	→	_____ _____
3. _____ _____	→	**He opened his umbrella.**

Name: _____

What Are Living Things?

Zebras

Some things in the world are alive. We call them **living** things. Plants and animals are living things.

Living things need air and water.

Seedling

Living things **grow** and **change**.

Mare and foal

Living things have young. They **reproduce**.

Directions: Circle the living things. Put an X on the nonliving things.

Name: _____

What Living Things Do

Living things **grow**. Living things **reproduce**. Living things **learn** and **change**.

| This baby kitten will grow up to be a cat. | This small plant will grow up to be a tree. | Big lions have little lion babies called cubs. |

| Plants make seeds that grow into new plants. | This child is learning to read and write numbers. | This dog is learning to jump! |

Directions: Use the bold words from the text to fill in the blanks.

1. Living things _____.

2. Living things _____.

3. Living things _____ and _____.

Name: _____

Living or Nonliving?

Directions: Here are two kinds of worms. Circle the correct answer for each question.

Gummy Worm

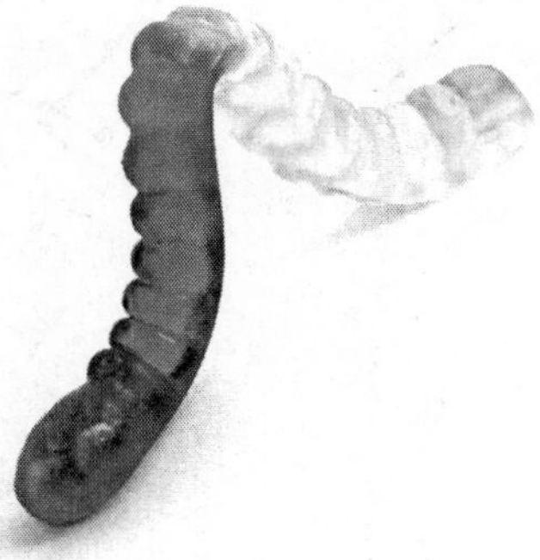

1. Does it grow?   yes   no

2. Does it need air?   yes   no

3. Does it move by itself?   yes   no

4. Can it learn and change?   yes   no

Earthworm

5. Does it grow?   yes   no

6. Does it need air?   yes   no

7. Does it move by itself?   yes   no

8. Can it learn and change?   yes   no

9. Which worm is living?   gummy worm   earthworm

10. Which worm is not living?   gummy worm   earthworm

Name: _____

Living and Nonliving Things Are Different

Living things grow and change.

They need air and water.

They can make more of themselves.

Family

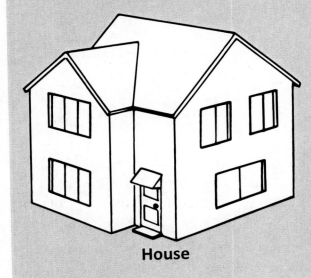

House

Nonliving things do not grow or move by themselves.

They do not need air or water.

They cannot make more of themselves.

1. Draw a living thing.

2. Draw a nonliving thing.

©*Teacher Created Resources*

Name: _____

Living and Nonliving Parts of a Habitat

➡ Plants and animals are **living** things.

➡ Rocks are **nonliving** things. They are not alive. Water is not alive. Dirt is not alive. Air is not alive.

Directions: Circle 5 living things you see in this picture. Draw an X on 3 nonliving things you see in this scene.

Name: _____

What Living Things Need

Animals need water. Plants need water.

Animals need air. Plants need air. Animals need to eat food.

Plants need sunlight. They use it to make food.

Directions: Fill in the chart to show what plants and animals need. Use ✓ marks.

	Air	Food	Sunlight	Water
Plants				
Animals				

Name: _____

Plant Needs

What do plants need to live and grow? Plants make their own food. Plants need light from the Sun to make food. They also need air and water. Without these things, they cannot live. They cannot grow.

Directions: Write each word in the Word Bank in the correct column.

1.

Word Bank	Plants	
	Need	**Do Not Need**
air		
nest		
rock		
Sun		
water		

2. How do plants get food? _____

_____

Name: _____

Animal Needs

What do animals need to live and grow? Animals need to eat food. Some eat plants. Some eat meat. Animals need water. They need air. They need shelter. **Shelter** is a safe place to live.

Directions: In each box, draw an animal getting what it needs.

Food	Shelter

Water

©*Teacher Created Resources*

Name: _____

Compare a Plant and an Animal

Directions: Write each need in the correct spot on the Venn diagram.

Word Bank	air	food	shelter	Sun	water

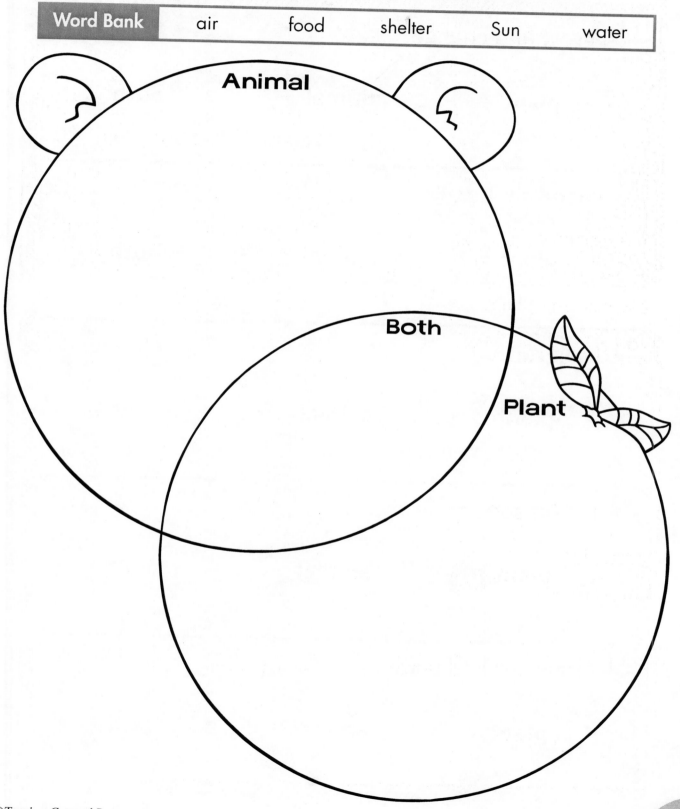

Name: _____

What Am I?

Directions: Read each sentence. Circle *plant*, *animal*, or *both*.

1 I grow and change.

plant   animal   **both**

2 I need shelter.

plant   animal   **both**

3 I can run.

plant   animal   **both**

4 I make food from the Sun.

plant   animal   **both**

5 I need air and water.

plant   animal   **both**

Name: _____

Plants Have Roots and Stems

Plants have **roots**. Roots grow down. They go into the ground. They hold the plant so it does not fall over. Roots bring water up to the plant.

We can eat some plant roots.

Carrot

Giant sequoia

Plants have **stems**. The stem holds the plant up. It carries water to the leaves. The stem of a tree is called the **trunk**.

We can eat some plant stems.

Celery

Asparagus

1. Roots grow _____.

2. Roots go into the _____.

3. Stems carry _____ to the leaves of a plant.

4. Draw roots and a stem. ⟶

Name: _____

Plants Have Leaves

Most plants have green **leaves**. The leaves take in sunlight. The leaves take in air. Leaves make food for the plant. Leaves can be big or small. They can be different shapes.

We can eat some plant leaves.

Lettuce   **Spinach**

1. Leaves take in _____

   and _____.

2. Leaves make _____ for the plant.

3. Draw some leaves.

Name: _____

Plants Have Flowers

Plants have **flowers**.

Flowers have **petals**.

Flowers make **fruits** and **seeds**.

Seeds make more plants.

Sunflower and seeds

We can eat some flowers.

Broccoli

Cauliflower

1. Flowers have colorful _____.

2. What color is your favorite flower? _____

3. Flowers make _____ to make more plants.

4. Draw a flower.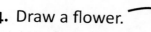

Name: _____

Plants Have Fruits and Seeds

Some plants have **fruits**. Fruits come from flowers. Fruits have **seeds** inside. New plants grow from seeds.

Apple blossoms

Apples

Apple seeds

We can eat many fruits.

Watermelons

Peaches

We can eat some seeds.

Corn kernels

Sunflower seeds

1. Fruits come from _____.

2. Fruits have _____ inside.

3. Seeds make new _____.

4. Draw your favorite fruit. ⟶

Name: _____

Parts of a Plant

Directions: Label the parts of a plant.

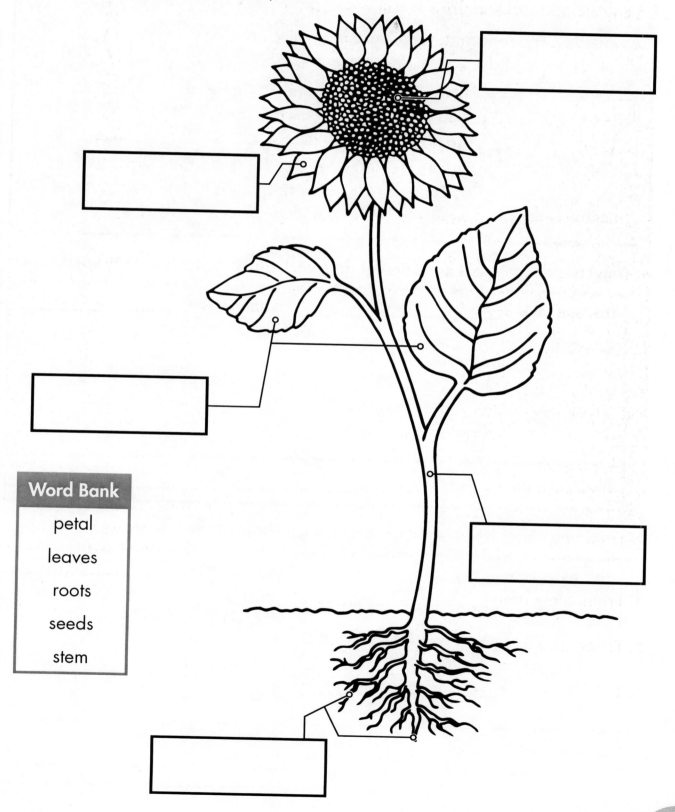

Word Bank

petal

leaves

roots

seeds

stem

Name: _____

Animals and Plants Are the Same and Different

Animals can be the same. They all grow and change. They all eat food and drink water.

Animals can be different. Bears are big. Mice are small. Fish live in the water. Dogs live on land.

Mouse and bear

Plants can be the same. They all have leaves. They all have roots.

Plants can be different. Trees are tall. Grass is short. A cactus can live where there is little water. Seaweed needs to live in the water.

Cactus and fern

1. Draw two animals that are different from each other. Write how they are different.

This animal is a _____ .   This animal is a _____ .

They are different because _____ .

2. Draw two plants that are different from each other. Write how they are different.

This plant is a _____ .   This plant is a _____ .

They are different because _____ .

Name: _____

We Are the Same and Different

People are all the same in some ways. We all eat food. We all breathe air. We all move and grow.

People can be different in some ways. They can be different ages or sizes. They can have different skin or hair colors. They can like different things.

Directions: Draw a picture of you and a friend.

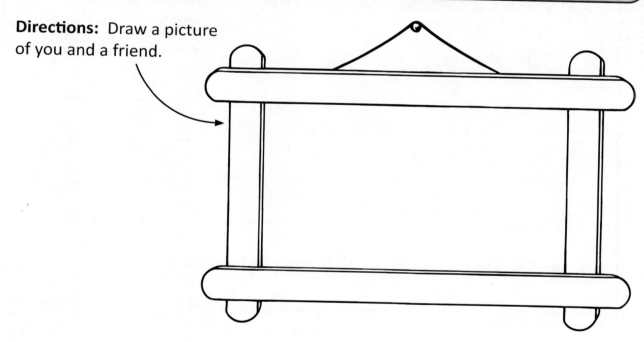

1. What is one way that you and your friend look the same? _____

_____

2. What is one way that you and your friend look different from each other?

_____

3. What is one thing that you both like? _____

4. What are some things that just one of you likes?

_____

Name: _____

Animals of the Same Kind

These animals are both bears. They are the same in some ways. They are different in other ways.

Brown bear

Giant panda

These bears are **different** in some ways. Brown bears have brown fur. They eat both plants and meat. They live where it is cold, so they sleep in the winter.

Giant pandas have black-and-white fur. They eat plants. They live where it is warmer, so they stay awake in the winter.

How are these bears the **same**? They both are big and have thick fur. They have large paws with long claws. The bears have little, round ears and short tails.

Directions: Fill in the chart below. Write ways that each bear is different. Then, write some ways they are the same.

Brown Bear	Giant Panda
Same	

Name: _____

Animals in the Same Family

These kittens are brothers and sisters. They have the same mother. The kittens look alike in some ways. They look different from one another, too.

1. How do these kittens look alike? _____

_____

_____

2. How do these kittens look different from one another? _____

_____

_____

Name: _____

Grouping Plants

This is a scientist. She studies plants. She wants to find out how plants are the same and different.

Directions: Help the scientist. Look at the plants. Answer the questions.

| Cactus | Rose | Strawberry |
| Grapes | Lettuce | Carrot |

1. Which plants have thorns? _____ _____

2. Which plants have flowers?

_____ _____

3. Which plants have fruit?

_____ _____

4. Which plants are vegetables? _____ _____

Name: _____

Mammals

Mammals are a kind of animal. Cats and dogs are mammals. How do we know if an animal is a mammal?

Hippopotamus

- Mammals have **hair** or **fur**. Some animals have thick fur. Some animals have hair. Even hippos and whales have a few hairs.
- Mammals have **lungs**. They breathe air.
- Mammals can live in the water, but they still need air. Whales and dolphins are mammals that get air through holes in the tops of their heads!

- Mammals are **warm-blooded**. Their bodies can heat up when it is cold. They can cool down when it is hot.
- Mammals have **backbones**.
- Mammals, such as cows and bats, feed their babies **milk**. Other kinds of animals cannot make milk.

Bison calf nursing

1. Circle the mammals. Put an X on the animals that are not mammals.

2. Are you a mammal?   **Yes**   **No**

How do you know? _____

_____

Name: _____

Insects

Have you seen small animals, such as ants or beetles? Have you seen flying bugs, such as bees? Many small animals are **insects**.

Insects have 3 body parts:

- The **head** is the first part.
  The head has **2 eyes**, **2 antennae**, and **1 mouth**.
- The **thorax** is the middle part.
  The **6 legs** come from the thorax.
  Most insects have **wings** on the thorax.
- The **abdomen** is the big part at the back.

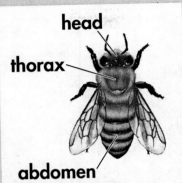

Insects do not have bones. They wear their skeletons on the outside of their bodies. Their skeletons are like shells.

Did you know? Not all small animals are insects.

 Spiders are not insects. They have 8 legs and 2 body parts.

Pill bugs are not insects. They have 14 legs.

1. Look at the ant. Draw a line from each word to the insect body part.

abdomen   head

            leg

thorax   antenna

2. How many legs does an insect have?   **4**   **6**   **8**

3. Circle the insects. Put an X on the animals that are not insects.

4. How did you decide which animals were insects? _____

_____

Name: _____

Fish

Fish live in water. Some fish live in freshwater lakes and rivers. Some fish live in the salt water of the ocean.

Fish have **gills**. They breathe in the water. They cannot live on land.

- Fish have **scales** on the outside of their bodies.
- Fish have **backbones**. They are **vertebrates**.
- Fish have **fins** and **tails** to help them swim.
- Fish are **cold-blooded**. They cannot warm themselves up or cool off.

gills

Not Fish

Not all animals that live underwater are fish.

- Octopuses are not fish. They do not have scales. They have many arms, but no fins. They do not have bones.
- Crabs are not fish. They have shells. They have legs.
- Jellyfish are not fish! They don't have bones or fins.
- Whales and dolphins look like fish, but they are not fish. They have lungs, not gills. They breathe air. They make milk for their babies.

1. Circle the fish. Put an X on the animals that are not fish.

2. Whales and dolphins are not fish. What kind of animals are they?

mammals   **birds**   **insects**

3. How did you decide if the animals were fish? _____

_____

Name: _____

Reptiles

Have you ever seen a snake or a lizard? How about a turtle? These animals are **reptiles**.

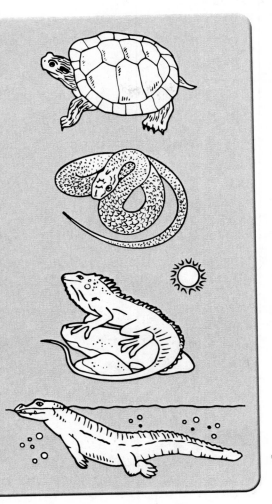

- Reptiles are covered in **scales**. Reptile scales don't grow. They fall off as the animal gets bigger. New, bigger scales grow in their place.

- Some reptiles, such as turtles, have **shells**.

- Scales and shells help keep reptiles safe.

- Reptiles are **vertebrates**. That means they have backbones.

- Most reptiles live where it is warm. They are **cold-blooded**. They need the Sun to warm them up.

- Reptiles have **lungs** and breathe air. Some live on land. Some live in the water. Sea turtles and crocodiles live in the water. There are even snakes that live in water!

Directions: Fill in the missing words. Use the Word Bank.

Word Bank	land	Sun	water	scales	lungs

1. Reptiles' bodies are covered in _____.

2. Reptiles need the _____ to warm up.

3. All reptiles breathe air with their _____.

4. Some reptiles live on _____, and some live in the _____.

5. What is your favorite reptile? _____

   Why? _____

   _____

Name: _____

Birds

Here is how you know that an animal is a bird.

- Birds' bodies are covered in **feathers**.
- Birds have **wings**. Most birds can fly, but some cannot.
  - ▶ Ostriches cannot fly, but they can run!
  - ▶ Penguins cannot fly, but they can swim!
- Birds breathe air with their **lungs**.
- Birds are **vertebrates**. They have backbones.
- Birds are **warm-blooded**.
- Birds lay **eggs**.

Did You Know?

Bats can fly, but they are *not* birds. Bats have fur and feed milk to their babies. What kind of animals are they?

Moths and butterflies have wings. They can fly, but they are not birds. They have six legs and antennae. What kind of animal are they?

Directions: Fill in the missing words.

Word Bank	eggs	birds	feathers	warm

1. Birds have _____ all over their bodies.

2. Pigeons and sparrows are _____.

3. Birds are _____-blooded.

4. Birds lay _____.

Directions: Circle **Yes** or **No**.

5. All birds can fly.   **Yes**   **No**

6. All animals that fly are birds.   **Yes**   **No**

Name: _____

Animal Senses

How do you learn about the world? You use parts of your body. You see with your eyes. You hear with your ears. Animals use their body parts to find out about the world, too.

Animals use their senses to find food.

Animals look for food with their eyes. Owls and cats can see in the dark. This helps them hunt. Bees can see colors in flowers that we can't see. They know which flowers have food.

Animals smell and taste food. Snakes use their tongues to catch smells of food in the air. Earthworms can taste all over their bodies!

Animals use their senses to stay safe.

Animals listen. They look for danger. Rabbits and deer see and hear when danger is coming. Dogs can smell when danger is near.

Animals use their senses to communicate.

Many animals use sounds to communicate, or "talk," to one another. Birds chirp. Dogs bark. Frogs croak.

Some animals use smells to send one another messages. Ants talk to one another by touching their antennae together.

Directions: Write the sense that each animal is using. Use the Word Bank.

Word Bank	smell	hearing	sight	taste	touch

1. An eagle sees a rabbit moving in the snow. _____

2. A rabbit hears something moving in the bushes. _____

3. A dog sniffs the air. _____

4. Butterflies can taste with their feet. _____

5. Ants rub their antennae together to talk. _____

Name: _____

Animal Movement

Some body parts help animals move from place to place.

Cheetahs are fast runners. They have strong **legs**. They run fast to catch their prey. The gazelles that they chase run fast, too!

Mountain goats use their legs and **hooves** to climb steep cliffs. They find plants to eat that other animals cannot get to. Predators cannot follow them.

Some animals have **wings**. Butterflies use their wings to fly from flower to flower to find food. Bats and owls fly fast to catch prey. Many birds fly a long way in winter to get to warm places.

Some animals swim with **fins** and **tails**. Sharks swim fast to catch their food. Small fish swim away from predators. Whales swim many miles to find warmer waters.

Directions: Match the animal to the way it moves.

Animal	Movement
	hop
	swim
	fly
	swing

Name: _____

Animals Eat and Drink

Eagle with fish

Some body parts help animals eat and drink.

Eagles swoop down on their food and catch it in their claws. They tear the food apart with their beaks.

Opossums hold food with their paws. They take small bites with their sharp teeth.

Parrots crack open fruits and seeds with their strong beaks.

Butterfly

Butterflies have mouthparts like straws. They poke them into flowers and sip the sweet food.

Giraffes have very long tongues. A giraffe can wrap its tongue around a branch. Then, it pulls off the leaves and eats them.

Elephant drinking

Animals drink water in different ways. Most animals lap up water with their tongues. Elephants suck up water with their trunks. They squirt the water into their mouths. Snakes rest their jaws in water and soak it up like a sponge.

Directions: Write how each animal will eat its food.

1. **parrot** _____

_____

2. **opossum** _____

_____

3. **giraffe** _____

_____

Name: _____

Animals Keep Warm or Cool

If you are cold, what can you do? You can put on a jacket. Animals have body parts to keep them warm or cool.

Feathers keep birds warm. When it gets cold, birds can fluff up their feathers. This traps air to keep them warm. Penguins can swim in freezing water because their feathers are waterproof.

Sheep have curly fur called **wool**. It keeps them very warm. When it gets hot, farmers shave most of the wool off so the sheep can cool down.

Some animals live where it is very cold. Polar bears have clear **fur**. The Sun shines through the fur onto their black skin. This warms them up. Whales and seals have fat called **blubber** under their skin. This is like a big, warm jacket. Blubber in whales can be two feet thick!

When you get hot, your body makes **sweat**. This helps keep you cool. Monkeys, apes, and horses also sweat to keep cool.

Have you ever seen a dog with its tongue hanging out? That helps the dog cool off when it is hot!

Directions: Use the Word Bank to help you fill in the blanks.

Word Bank	fur	blubber	sweat	feathers	wool

1. Birds can fluff up their _____ to keep warm.

2. Polar bears have clear _____ and black skin to stay warm.

3. A sheep's warm fur is called _____.

4. Horses _____ to keep cool.

5. Whales have _____ under their skin to keep them warm.

Name: _____

Animals Protect Themselves

Some **body parts** help keep animals safe. The outside of an animal's body can help keep it safe.

- ▶ Snails can pull their bodies into their shells.
- ▶ Porcupines have sharp quills all over their bodies.
- ▶ Pangolins have hard scales. They can roll up into a ball.

Porcupine

An animal's coloring can help keep it safe.

- ▶ A zebra's stripes help it blend into the tall grasses.
- ▶ Some lizards can change their colors to hide.
- ▶ Some insects look like sticks or leaves.
- ▶ The bright colors of some poisonous frogs send a warning. It would be a bad idea to eat them!

Pangolin

Some animals have odd body parts to keep them safe.

Kangaroo and joey

- ▶ Skunks can spray a very bad smell. This chases predators away.
- ▶ Rattlesnakes make a sound when they shake their tails. This warns everyone to stay away!
- ▶ A mother kangaroo has a pouch. Her baby can go inside and stay safe.

Directions: Choose an animal you read about. Think about how it uses a body part to stay safe. How could you copy this idea to make something to keep *you* safe? Draw your idea.

Animal: _____

Body Part: _____

My Idea: _____

_____

Name: _____

Plants Reproduce

All living things **reproduce**. *Reproduce* means "to make new life." Animals make new life by having babies. How do plants reproduce?

Most plants make seeds. Seeds grow from flowers. You can find seeds inside fruits and nuts.

Each seed has a baby plant inside. The baby plant grows when the seed gets what it needs.

Each kind of plant makes new plants of its own kind.

▶ Apple seeds make new apple trees.

▶ Rose seeds make new rosebushes.

▶ Watermelon seeds grow into watermelon vines.

1. *Reproduce* means

   _____.

   a. to grow

   b. to make new life

   c. inside fruit

2. What do seeds do?

   a. grow new plants

   b. make baby animals

   c. grow on leaves

3. An apple seed can grow into

   _____.

   a. a pineapple plant

   b. an ivy plant

   c. an apple tree

Name: _____

Seeds

Why do plants have flowers? Flowers make fruits and seeds! Flowers have pretty colors that attract insects. Insects, such as bees, help the flowers make fruits and seeds.

Seed Parts

▶ A seed has a **seed coat** on the outside. It protects the seed.

▶ The **embryo** is the baby plant.

▶ Most of the seed is **food** for the baby plant as it grows.

What is a seed for? Inside each seed is a baby plant ready to grow.

When a seed gets what it needs, the baby plant inside begins to grow. It pushes out of the seed. The plant grows toward the light.

1. What is a flower's job?

   a. To be picked for a vase.

   b. To make the air smell nice.

   c. To make fruits and seeds.

2. The _____ protects the seed.

3. Most of the seed is _____ for the baby plant.

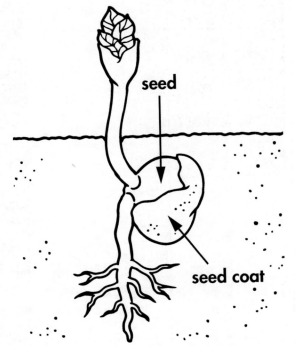

seed

seed coat

Name: _____

Seeds Move

Seeds need to leave their parent plant and find a new home. They need water and sunlight. They need a place with space to grow.

Some seeds find a new home with help from animals. A seed can **stick to an animal's fur**. It goes for a ride. It falls off in a new place. If the seed gets what it needs, it will grow a new plant.

Animals like to eat fruits. Sometimes, they eat the seeds, too. The animal moves to a new place. The seeds go **through the animal and come out again**. The seeds may grow in the new place.

Some seeds find a new home with help from the wind. Dandelion seeds have fluff on them. They **fly** in the wind.

Maple seeds look like little helicopters. They spin through the air.

Water can help seeds move, too. Some seeds fall into a river or a stream. They **float** to a new place.

Some seeds move by **exploding**! This kind of seed grows in a pod. When the seeds are ready, the pod pops open. The seeds fly out.

1. Why do seeds need to move away from the plant they grew on?
   a. They need space to grow.
   b. They need to stick to an animal.
   c. They want their own place.

Maple seed

2. How do maple seeds travel? _____

3. What are two other ways that seeds can travel?

_____

_____

Name: _____

Match the Plant to Its Parent

Plants reproduce. The new plant looks like the parent plant.

Directions: Draw a line from each small plant to its parent plant.

Strawberry plant

Oak seedling

Grass

Cactus

Name: _____

Growing a Plant

Callum was helping his uncle in the garden. He dug a small hole. He put in a seed. He covered the seed with soil. He sprinkled some water over the soil.

Callum wondered what kind of plant would grow from the seed. Every day, he looked. One day, a small seedling poked out of the soil. Callum gave the plant water. Every day, it grew bigger.

One day, a flower grew on the plant. But Callum still couldn't tell what kind of plant it was.

The flower grew bigger. Then, it started to change. The petals fell off. A fruit began to grow.

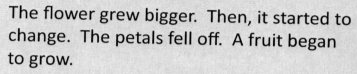

Finally, Callum knew what kind of plant it was. When the berries were ready, he picked them. They tasted so good!

1. What kind of plant did Callum grow?
   a. an apple tree   **b.** a carrot plant   **c.** a strawberry plant

2. What did Callum do in this story?

First, he _____.

Then, he _____.

Finally, he _____.

Name: _____

Animals Reproduce

Giraffe family

All living things **reproduce**. *Reproduce* means "to make new life." Animals make new life when they have babies.

Some babies look like their parents. Baby giraffes look like adult giraffes. They are smaller than their parents. Baby snakes look like small adult snakes.

Some babies do **not** look like their parents.

Tadpoles are frog babies. They do not look like frogs!

Tadpole   **Frog**

Caterpillars are butterfly babies. They do not look like butterflies!

Caterpillar   **Butterfly**

These babies change as they grow. They will look like their parents when they are adults.

1. What does *reproduce* mean? _____

_____

2. Draw an animal parent and baby.

   What animal did you draw?

   _____

3. Do they look alike?   **Yes**   **No**

Name: _____

Live Babies or Eggs?

How are animal babies born? Do their parents take care of them?

Some animals have live babies. The babies grow inside the mother. When they are ready, they are born.

Almost all mammals give birth to live babies. The mother gives the babies milk. They take care of their babies until they are big enough to take care of themselves.

Lemur family

Alligator hatchling

Some animals lay eggs. The babies grow inside the eggs. When they are ready, they **hatch**. *Hatch* means "to come out of an egg."

Most reptiles lay eggs. When the babies hatch, they take care of themselves.

Most fish lay eggs. Some leave the eggs. The babies take care of themselves. Other fish make nests. They take care of their eggs. They take care of their babies.

Birds lay eggs. They make a nest or a safe place. They take care of the eggs. They keep them warm. When the babies are born, the parents feed them. They take care of them until they are big enough to take care of themselves.

Bird feeding babies

1. *Hatch* means _____.
   - **a.** to be born
   - **b.** to make a nest
   - **c.** to come out of an egg

2. What is one kind of animal that lays eggs? _____

3. What is one kind of animal that has live babies? _____

Name: _____

Babies That Look Like Their Parents

Bear with cubs

Some babies look like their parents. Baby birds and mammals look a lot like their parents. They have the same body parts. They are just smaller. Look at the bear and her cubs.

Some babies might be a different color from their parents. They might not have all their feathers or fur. But, they have the same body shape.

Duck family

Mammal and bird babies cannot take care of themselves. The parents must feed them. They must keep the babies safe.

Baby sea turtles

Some reptiles look like their parents. Sea turtles do. The parents do not have to take care of the babies. The babies can feed themselves. They know how to hide or run from danger.

Directions: Look at the photo of the mother and baby horse. Answer the questions.

1. How do the mother and baby look alike?

   _____

   _____

2. How do they look different from each other?

   _____

   _____

Mare and foal

Name: _____

A Lot in Common

Directions: Look at the swan and her babies.

Swan with cygnets

1. What is the *same* about the mother swan and her babies? _____

   _____

2. What is *different*? _____

   _____

Directions: Draw an adult animal and its baby. Choose an animal that has babies that look like the parents.

3. What is the *same* about the parent

   and baby? _____

   _____

   _____

4. What is *different* about the parent

   and the baby? _____

   _____

   _____

Name: _____

Babies That Change to Look Like Their Parents

Some babies do not look like their parents. They change as they grow. When they are adults, they will look like their parents.

Moths lay **eggs**. **Caterpillars** hatch from the eggs. Caterpillars eat leaves. They grow bigger.

When they are big enough, the caterpillars wrap themselves up. They make **cocoons**.

They change while they are inside. When they finish changing, they come out. The caterpillar is now a **moth**!

Silkworm cocoon

Silkworm moth adult

Silkworm caterpillar

Directions: Label the stages of the moth life cycle.

| Word Bank | eggs | caterpillar | cocoon | moth |

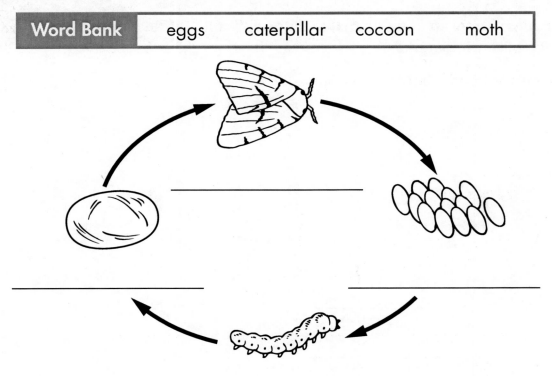

Name: _____

Animals Take Care of Their Offspring

Many animals take care of their **offspring**. *Offspring* means "children" or "babies."

➡ Animals make safe homes. Some dig dens. Some build nests.

➡ Some feed their babies milk. Many animals bring food to their babies.

➡ They keep them warm. They hide them from danger.

Young animals also do things to help themselves.

➡ They cry when they are hungry.

➡ They hide or run from danger.

Gorilla with baby

Stork feeding babies

Owlets hiding

1. What are *offspring*?
   a. parents   **b.** animals   **c.** babies

2. Who takes care of you? What do they do to help you?

   _____

   _____

3. How do you help take care of yourself?

   _____

   _____

Name: _____

Animals Prepare for Their Offspring

Many animals **prepare** to have offspring. *Prepare* means "to get ready."

A polar bear mother digs into the snow. She makes a warm space. She will have her babies in her den. They will be safe inside.

Polar bear with cubs

An octopus finds a safe place to lay her eggs. Then, she stays with the eggs. She cleans the eggs. She blows water over the eggs. She chases away animals that would eat her eggs.

Bald eagles in a nest

A pair of eagles builds a nest. They choose a tall tree. They gather sticks. They put the sticks together to make a nest. The mother lays eggs in the nest. The mother and the father take turns sitting on the eggs. This keeps the eggs warm. When the eggs hatch, the baby eagles will be safe in the nest.

1. *Prepare* means _____.
   a. to protect babies   **b.** to sit on eggs   **c.** to get ready

2. How do eagles prepare for their offspring?
   a. They build a nest.
   b. They blow water.
   c. They dig in the snow.

3. How does a mother polar bear prepare for her babies to be born?

   _____

   _____

Name: _____

Animals Protect Their Offspring

Animal parents **protect** their offspring. *Protect* means "to keep safe."

Animals keep their babies warm.

- Baby birds stay warm under their parents' feathers.
- Penguins hold their babies on top of their feet.

Emperor penguins with chicks

Opossum carrying young

Some animals live in herds.

- Elephants live together. They help take care of all the babies. They keep them safe. They scare away other animals.

Some animals carry their offspring to keep them safe.

- Baby alligators ride in their mother's mouth. Her sharp teeth protect them.

- Baby opossums ride on their mother's backs.
- Kangaroo mothers have a pouch. It is like a big, soft pocket. The babies ride inside.
- Cats can't carry their babies with their paws. They grab their necks with their mouths. It does not hurt them.

Tiger carrying cub

1. Which word means "to keep safe"?
   a. protect   **b.** offspring   **c.** pouch

2. How do elephants protect their offspring? _____

_____

3. What is one way animals carry their offspring? _____

_____

Name: _____

Animals Feed Their Offspring

Animals feed their offspring. Some bring food to their babies. Some teach their babies how to find food.

Elk calf nursing

Some animals feed their babies.

- Mammal mothers give milk to their babies. The babies drink milk until they get bigger. Then, they can eat food like their mothers.
- Fox mothers catch prey. They bring it to their babies to eat.
- Birds catch fish and worms. They bring the food to their babies.

Animal parents must teach their offspring to find food.

- Mother elephants teach their babies how to grab food with their trunks. Then, they use their trunks to put the food into their mouths.
- Mother cheetahs show their children how to hunt.

Mother cheetah with cubs

1. Mammal mothers give _____ to their babies.
   a. meat   **b.** milk   **c.** fruit

2. Some animal parents _____ their babies to find food.
   a. push   **b.** grab   **c.** teach

3. What is one way an animal feeds its baby? _____

_____

Name: _____

Young Animals Help Themselves

Some animals need help when they are born. Other babies can help themselves.

Some babies make noise when they are hungry. Baby birds make loud sounds. The parents bring food to the nest. The babies open their mouths and eat.

Each zebra is part of a **herd**. A *herd* is a big group of animals. Baby zebras can run very soon after they are born. They will be safer if they run with the other zebras.

Some animal babies must hide to be safe. Adult meerkats make a sound when danger is near. Young meerkats hear the sound. They run into tunnels and hide.

1. A *herd* is a _____ .

    a. a big group of animals   **b.** a nest of baby birds   **c.** a meerkat family

2. Draw a line to match the animal to what it does to stay safe.

    (It hides.)   (It makes noise.)   (It runs.)

Name: _____

Animals Live in Habitats

The place where an animal lives is called its **habitat**. Animals find food and water there. They find shelter in their habitat.

Arctic hare

Animals are **adapted** to live in one habitat. That means they have body parts that help them live in that place. They do things that help them live in that place.

Arctic hares and jackrabbits look alike. But they are adapted to live in different habitats.

Arctic hares live where it snows in the winter. When it gets cold, their fur turns white. This makes it hard for predators to see them. Their white fur is thick. It keeps them warm. They can dig in the snow to find plants to eat.

Jackrabbit

Jackrabbits live where it is hot. Their fur is the color of sand. This makes it hard for predators to see them. They stay in the shade during the hot part of the day. They go out to find food at night. They get water from the plants they eat.

1. The place where an animal lives is its _____.
   a. predator   **b.** habitat   **c.** shelter

2. Arctic hares live where it is _____ in the winter.
   a. cold   **b.** warm   **c.** hot

3. What is one way jackrabbits are adapted to live where it is hot?

   _____

   _____

   _____

Name: _____

Desert Habitat

The desert is a dry habitat. It is hot. There is not much water. The animals that live there must be able to live in the heat. They must be able to live with very little water.

Some animals, such as kit foxes, dig dens in the ground. Tortoises dig homes in the ground, too. It is cooler there. They hide in their homes all day. This keeps them cool. They come out at night. They look for food to eat.

Desert tortoise burrow

Chameleon eating beetle

It is hard for desert animals to get water. Desert plants have a lot of water in their leaves and stems. Animals can get water by eating these plants. Animals that eat other animals get water from the meat.

1. In the desert, there is not very much _____.
   a. food
   b. water
   c. sunlight

2. Circle the 3 animals that are *adapted* to live in a desert habitat.
   Put an X on the animals that do not live in the desert.

Name: _____

Rainforest Habitat

Sloth

Rainforests are wet and warm all year long. Many different plants and animals live there. The animals do not get cold. They can find a lot of food.

Sloths live in the trees. They move very slowly. They have to hide to be safe. Sloths have little, green plants growing flat on their fur. The plants make them look like they are part of the rainforest.

Toucan

Many animals in the rainforest eat plants. Each animal has a special way to get its food. Toucans have very long beaks. They can reach fruit that other animals cannot reach.

Snake in a tree

Many rainforest animals are small. It is easy for them to move between all the trees and plants. Snakes in the rainforest can get very big. It is easy for them to slither through the trees to get food.

1. Rainforests are always _____ and warm.
   a. cold   **b.** wet   **c.** loud

2. Circle the 3 animals that are *adapted* to live in the trees of the rainforest.
   Put an X on the animals that do not live in the trees of the rainforest.

Name: _____

Polar Habitat

Polar habitats are very cold. There are not many plants. There is a lot of snow and ice. Animals that live there must be able to live in the cold. They must be able to find food on the ice or in the water. They must **adapt** to the weather.

Polar bears are adapted to live in the cold. Their fur is clear. The Sun shines through it. It warms the dark skin underneath.

Polar bear

Polar bears can swim in very cold water. They can walk a long way on the ice. They look for seals to eat.

Walrus

Seals, whales, and walruses have a special fat called *blubber* all over their bodies. This fat keeps them warm on the ice and in the cold water. They are good at diving to catch fish to eat.

1. Which of these is a polar habitat?
   a. It is cold. There are not many plants.
   b. It is warm. There are a lot of trees.
   c. It is hot. There are not many plants.

2. Circle the 3 animals that are *adapted* to live in a polar habitat.

   Put an X on the animals that do not live in a polar habitat.

Name: _____

Ocean Habitat

An ocean habitat is under the water. The animals that live there must breathe underwater. They must move underwater. They must be able to find food in the water.

Shark

Sharks are adapted to live in the ocean. They have gills to breathe in the water. They have fins and tails to swim. They have sharp teeth. They swim fast to catch prey.

Sea stars are adapted to live in the ocean. They do not need to breathe air. They get oxygen from the water through their feet. They don't have any blood. They pump the water through their bodies. They have many sticky feet to crawl on the ocean floor.

Sea star

1. Animals that live in the ocean must be able to _____.
   a. breathe underwater
   b. find food in the water
   c. both **a** and **b**

2. Circle the 3 animals that are *adapted* to live in an ocean habitat.

   Put an X on the animals that do not live in the ocean.

Name: _____

How Do You Get Energy?

Energy is how things change and move. You use energy to run and to play. You use energy to read and to write. You use energy to grow.

Where do you get your energy?

➡ You get energy from the food you eat.

Where does the energy in your food come from?

Vegetables

Chickens

➡ All energy on Earth comes from the Sun.

➡ Plants use energy from the Sun to make their own food.

What happens when you eat a plant?

➡ You get the energy from that plant!

Have you ever eaten eggs or chicken?

➡ If you eat part of an animal, you get energy from that animal. The animal got its energy from the Sun.

---

1. You get _____ from the food you eat.
   a. energy   **b.** shelter

2. Plants use energy from the _____ to make their own food.

3. What did you eat to get energy today?

_____

_____

Name: _____

Animals Need Energy

All living things need energy. They need energy to live. They need energy to grow.

Plants get energy from the Sun. They use the Sun's energy to make food in their leaves. They use this food to live and grow.

All animals must eat food to get energy. Many animals eat plants.

Rabbits, zebras, and deer eat plants. They get energy from the plants. They use that energy to live and grow.

Rabbit eating grass

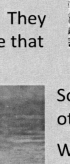

Cormorants fishing

Some animals eat the meat of other animals.

Wolves, lions, and owls eat meat. They get energy from the meat. They use that energy to live and grow.

Some animals eat both plants and meat. Bears, pigs, and skunks eat plants and meat. They get their energy from both!

Directions: Fill in the missing words.

1. Plants get energy from the _____.

2. All animals must eat _____ to get energy.

3. Some animals eat both _____ and _____.

Name: _____

What Is a Food Chain?

A **food chain** shows how energy moves.

All plants get their energy from the Sun.

This plant gets its energy from the Sun.

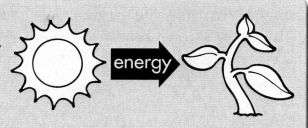

Some animals eat plants. They get energy from the plants.

This rabbit gets its energy from eating the plant.

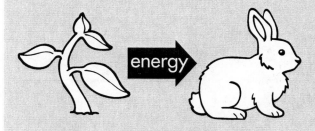

Some animals eat other animals. They get their energy from the meat.

This fox gets its energy from eating the rabbit.

This food chain shows how the energy moves from the Sun to the fox.

1. A *food chain* shows how _____ moves.
   a. an animal   **b.** a plant   **c.** energy

2. Draw in the arrows to show how the energy moves.

Name: _____

Finish the Food Chains

Directions: Draw the arrows in each food chain to show how the energy moves.

Directions: Fill in the missing words.

Word Bank	frog	snail	Sun

4. The plant gets energy from the _____.

5. The _____ gets energy from eating the snail.

6. The _____ gets energy from eating the plant.

Name: _____

What's Missing?

Directions: Look at each food chain. Draw the missing part. Explain each chain.

1. Sun   grass   mouse   hawk

2. Sun   grass   zebra   lion

3. Sun   kelp   sea urchin   sea otter

4. Sun   corn   chicken   fox

Name: _____

Our Senses

Your teacher is talking to the class. How do you know what she is saying? You hear her voice with your ears. Your ears send the message to your brain. Your brain knows what the teacher is saying.

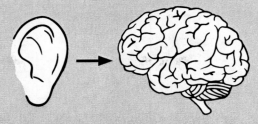

We have five senses. They each help us find out about the world around us.

	You **hear** with your ears. You can hear loud sounds such as fireworks. You can hear soft sounds such as whispers.
	You **see** with your eyes. You can see bright things such as light bulbs. You can see colors such as blue and red.
	You **smell** with your nose. You can smell nice things such as cookies. You can smell yucky things such as skunks.
	You **taste** with your tongue. You can taste sweet things such as apples. You can taste sour things such as lemons.
	You **feel** with your skin. You can feel things that are soft such as blankets. You can feel things that are hot and cold.

Directions: Fill in the blanks with things you like.

1. I see _____ with my eyes.

2. I hear _____ with my ears.

3. I smell _____ with my nose.

4. I taste _____ with my tongue.

5. I feel _____ with my skin.

Name: _____

Senses Keep Us Safe

Why do we have senses? We use our senses to find out about the world around us.

How do senses work? We use different body parts to sense things. Then, our brain tells us about them.

You can use your eyes to see an apple. Your eyes send a message to your brain. Your brain makes sense of what you see. It tells you, "That is an apple."

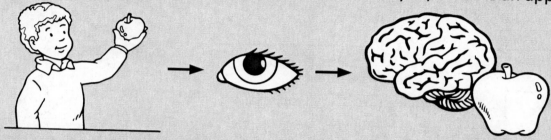

Our senses work with our brains to keep us safe.

➡ If you feel something hot, your brain tells you to pull your hand away.

➡ If you smell sour milk, your brain tells you not to drink it.

Directions: For each sense, fill in what your brain would tell you.

1. My eyes see a kitten. My brain tells me _____

   _____.

2. My nose smells smoke. My brain tells me _____

   _____.

3. My ears hear the teacher talking. My brain tells me _____

   _____.

4. My tongue tastes a carrot. My brain tells me _____

   _____.

5. My fingers feel a marble. My brain tells me _____

   _____.

Name: _____

Using More Than One Sense

We can use more than one sense to find out about some things. If you want to find out about a cookie, which senses could you use?

- You can **see** it with your eyes.
- You can **smell** it with your nose.
- You can **feel** it with your fingers.
- You can **taste** it with your tongue.
- You can even **hear** yourself chewing it!

DO NOT TOUCH Be careful using your senses.

Do not taste things that might be bad for you!

Do not touch very hot or sharp things that can hurt you!

Directions: Look at each item. Make an X in the box for each sense you would use to find out about it.

Which Senses Would You Use?					
	Sight	**Hearing**	**Smell**	**Taste**	**Touch**
cat					
hot dog					
xylophone					
TV					

Name: _____

Our Sense of Touch

We feel things through our skin. When you touch something, your skin sends a signal to your brain. Your brain knows what you are touching.

We use special words to talk about how something feels. The way something feels when you touch it is called its **texture**.

A blanket has a *soft* texture.

The bark of a tree has a *rough* texture.

We can also feel hot and cold. If we touch something cold, our skin sends a message to our brain. Our brain tells us it is cold.

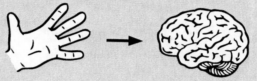

We don't just use our hands and fingers to feel things.

Our skin can send messages to our brain:

- You can feel the warm sunshine on your skin.
- You can feel a cold wind blowing over you.
- You can feel the grass underneath your bare feet.
- You can feel the softness of a shirt you are wearing.

1. Circle the words that describe what you might **feel** when you touch something.

blue	bright	cold
large	loud	rough	small
smooth	stinky	warm

2. Write a word to describe how each of these things would feel if you touched it.

 puppy   **pineapple**   **ice cube**

_____   _____   _____

Name: _____

Our Sense of Taste

Do you like the taste of sugar? Do you like the taste of salt? How do you know what they taste like?

We taste with our tongues. When you put something in your mouth, your tongue sends a message to your brain. Your brain tells you what you are tasting.

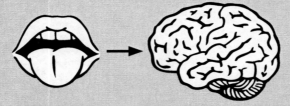

There are some things we should **never** taste. They might be too hot and burn us. They might be poison and make us sick. We can use our eyes, ears, and nose to find out if something is safe to taste. If you are not sure about something, do not put it in your mouth!

1. Circle the things you can taste. Put an X on the things you should not taste.

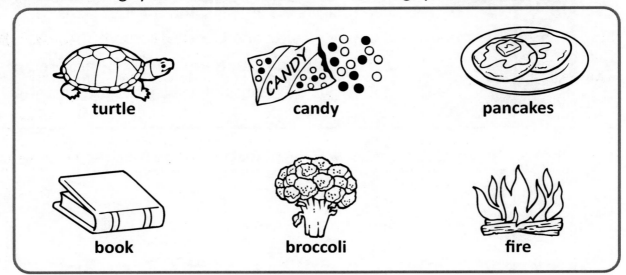

| turtle | candy | pancakes |
| book | broccoli | fire |

2. What are some tastes that you like?

_____ _____ _____

3. What are some tastes that you do **not** like?

_____ _____ _____

Name: _____

Day and Night

What is a **pattern**? A pattern happens over and over the same way. You can tell what comes next.

Day and night is a pattern. The Sun shines on Earth every day. It gets dark every night. It happens over and over in the same way.

Directions: Finish each pattern.

1. A B A B A ____

2. X O X O X ____ ____

3.   ____ ____

4.   ____ ____

5. Think about day and night. Then, draw something you do during the day and something you do at night.

Day 	Night 

Name: _____

Day and Night Skies

The sky at night looks different from the sky in the daytime.

In the daytime, the sky is light. We might see clouds. We see birds flying.

In the nighttime, the sky is dark. We can see the Moon. We might see stars.

Some things can be in the sky at any time. Clouds can be in the sky in the daytime or at night. Sometimes, we can see the Moon in the daytime.

Directions: Write each word in the Word Bank in the correct place in the diagram.

Word Bank	plane	clouds	Moon	rainbow	stars
	bat	lightning	owl	lizard	Sun

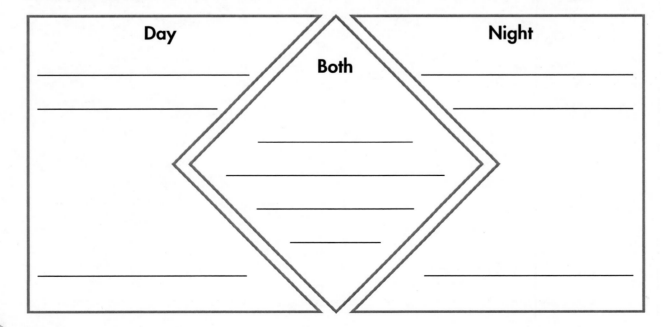

Day

Night

Both

Name: _____

The Sun

The Sun is a star. It is made of hot gases. The Sun makes light and heat. The Sun is much bigger than Earth. A million Earths could fit inside the Sun! It looks small because it is very far away.

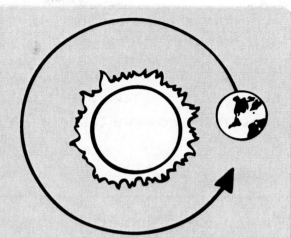

Earth goes around the Sun in a big oval path. It takes a year for Earth to go around the Sun.

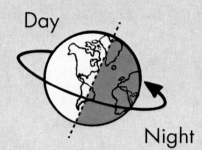

Day

Night

Earth also **spins**. It spins all the way around one time each day. When it is daytime, your place on Earth is facing the Sun. When it is nighttime, your place on Earth is facing away from the Sun.

Living things need the Sun. It warms Earth. Without the Sun, it would be too cold to live.

Plants need the Sun. They use sunlight to make food.

1. What is the Sun made of?
    a. solid rock   **b.** hot gases

2. We have day and night because Earth _____.
    a. spins   **b.** rests

3. Why do people on Earth need the Sun?

_____

_____

_____

Name: _____

The Moon

The Moon is made of rock. It is covered in dust. It has a lot of dents all over it.

The Moon is smaller than Earth. It is very far away. The Moon goes around Earth. It takes about one month for the Moon to go all the way around Earth.

The Moon does not make its own light. It **reflects** light from the Sun. *Reflect* means "to bounce off something." The Sun's light bounces off the Moon, and we can see it.

When we look at the Moon, it does not always look the same. Sometimes, it looks round. Sometimes, it looks like half a circle. Sometimes, it is shaped like a banana.

The Moon does not change shape. It is always round. We only see the part of the Moon the Sun is shining on.

1. The Moon is _____ than Earth.

   a. bigger   **b.** smaller

2. The Moon reflects light from the Sun. What does *reflect* mean?

   a. to shine   **b.** to bounce off something

3. Why does it look as if the Moon changes shape?

   _____

   _____

Name: _____

Astronauts

Astronauts go into space. Space is out past the air around Earth. Space is a dangerous place for people. There is no air. It gets very hot and very cold.

Spacecraft are machines. They are made to go into space. They keep the astronauts safe. It takes a lot of energy to make them go. Rockets push the spacecraft away from Earth.

Space shuttle launch

Astronauts must wear **space suits** in space. The suits give them air to breathe. They keep them cool or warm.

Astronauts have to be strong. They must be good at solving problems.

Astronaut in a space suit

2017 NASA astronaut class

1. Astronauts are people who travel to _____.
   a. the air   **b.** space   **c.** Earth

2. Astronauts must wear _____ _____ in space.

3. Why is space dangerous for people?

   _____

   _____

Name: _____

Four Seasons

Every year has four **seasons**:

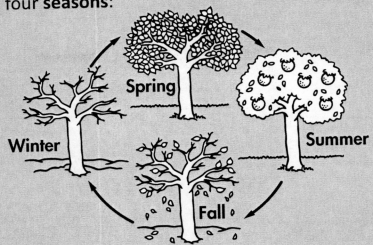

❄ **Winter** is the coldest season. The days are short. Plants stop growing. It snows in places that get very cold. People like to make snowmen. They drink hot cocoa.

❀ In **spring** the days get longer. The weather gets warmer. It rains a lot. Plants grow new leaves. Flowers bloom. People plant gardens.

☀ **Summer** is the hottest season. The days are long. The weather is hot and sunny. In summer, trees have many leaves. People like to go swimming.

🍃 In **fall**, the weather gets cooler. The days get shorter. The wind blows. Leaves fall off the trees. People wear sweaters.

Directions: Fill in the missing parts of the chart.

Season	Weather	Plants
	coldest	Plants stop growing.
Spring	warmer	
Summer		Plants have lots of leaves.
Fall	cooler	Leaves fall off trees.

Name: _____

Summer

Summer is the hottest season. The days are long. The nights are short.

The weather is hot and sunny. Sometimes, there are storms. You see lightning. You hear thunder.

In summer, plants have lots of leaves. It is nice to sit in the shade of a tree.

Animals find a lot of food in summer. Baby animals grow bigger. Bugs buzz around plants.

Because it is hot, you can wear shorts. It is fun to go swimming. Some families go on trips.

The Fourth of July is in summer. It is the birthday of America. We wear red, white, and blue. We watch fireworks.

1. Summer is the _____ season.
   a. coldest   **b.** hottest

2. What holiday takes place during the summer?
   a. Thanksgiving   **b.** the Fourth of July

3. What is one thing animals do in the summer? _____

_____

4. What do you like to do in the summer? _____

_____

Name: _____

Fall

Fall comes after summer. The days get shorter. The weather gets cooler. The wind blows.

Leaves turn yellow and orange. They fall off the trees. It is fun to play in a pile of leaves!

Animals gather food. They get ready for winter. Some birds fly away to warmer places.

Fall is cooler. We wear long sleeves. We wear sweaters. People pick apples and pumpkins.

Thanksgiving is in the fall. Families get together. They share a big dinner.

1. In fall, the days get _____.

    a. shorter

    b. longer

2. Some birds fly away to _____ places.

    a. colder

    b. warmer

3. In the box, draw what you would wear on a cool fall day. ⟶

A Fall Day

Name: _____

Winter

Winter comes after fall. The days are short. It gets dark early. The nights are long.

Winter weather is cold. In some places, it snows. We must be careful not to slip on ice.

In some places, plants do not grow in winter. Many trees have no leaves in winter.

Some animals sleep in the winter. They stay in their dens. It is too cold to go out. Some animals have thick fur to keep warm. They look for food in the snow.

We wear warm clothes in winter. We need warm coats. Sometimes, we wear hats and gloves.

Some people celebrate the New Year in winter. Some people stay up late. They hug one another when the new year begins.

1. Winter comes after _____.
   a. spring
   b. fall

2. We celebrate the _____ in winter.
   a. New Year
   b. Fourth of July

3. What are two things animals do in the winter?

_____

_____

Name: _____

Spring

Spring comes after winter. It starts to get warmer. The days get a little longer.

Spring weather can be cool and cloudy. It rains.

Plants start to grow in spring. The ground is no longer frozen. Plants get water from the rain. They grow new leaves. Flowers bloom. People plant gardens.

Sleeping animals wake up. They come out to look for food. Birds hatch from eggs. Baby animals are born.

In spring, we might need umbrellas. We wear raincoats. We wear rain boots.

Earth Day is in spring. People help clean up Earth. They plant new trees. They make it nice for all the plants and animals.

1. In spring, the days get a little _____.

   a. shorter

   b. longer

2. Baby animals are _____ in the spring.

3. Why do plants grow in the spring?

   _____

   _____

Name: _____

Types of Weather

Weather is what is going on in the air around us.

 When the air moves, we say it is **windy**.

 When the Sun is shining, we say it is **sunny**.

 When clouds are in the sky, we say it is **cloudy**.

 When rain falls down on us, we say it is **rainy**.

 When snow falls, we say it is **snowy**.

Directions: Write the best weather word for each picture.

Word Bank	sunny	rainy	snowy	windy

_____

_____

_____

_____

Name: _____

Dressing for the Weather

Do you look at the weather when you get dressed? It is important to wear the right clothes for the weather.

➡ **What do you wear if it is cold?**   ➡ **What do you wear if it is hot?**

Directions

1. Circle 5 things you can wear on a sunny day.

2. Draw a line under 3 things you would need on a rainy day.

3. Put an X on 5 things you could wear on a cold day.

Name: _____

What Would You Do?

Do you like to play outside? We can do different things in different kinds of weather.

What kind of weather is in the picture to the right? It is snowy weather. It is cold. Snow is falling. Sam is riding a saucer. It goes fast on the snow.

What kind of weather is in the picture below? It is windy weather. The air is moving fast. Joni is flying a kite. The wind helps the kite fly.

Directions: Draw yourself in each kind of weather. Write what you are doing.

Rainy Weather	**Sunny Weather**

Name: _____

Read a Weather Forecast

This is a weather **forecast**. It tells us what the weather will be like.

Monday	Tuesday	Wednesday	Thursday	Friday
Sunny	Snowy	Windy	Rainy	Cloudy

1. What will the weather be like on Tuesday? _____

2. On which day will you need an umbrella? _____

3. On which day will it be cloudy? _____

Directions: Use the statements below to draw and label the weather in each box.

4. It will be **cloudy** on Monday and Tuesday.

5. It will **snow** on Wednesday.

6. **Rain** will come on Thursday.

7. It will be **windy** on Friday.

Monday	Tuesday	Wednesday	Thursday	Friday

Name: _____

Weather Chart

Mrs. Ray's class was studying the weather. They wrote down the kind of weather they had each day. They made a graph to show the kinds of weather they had.

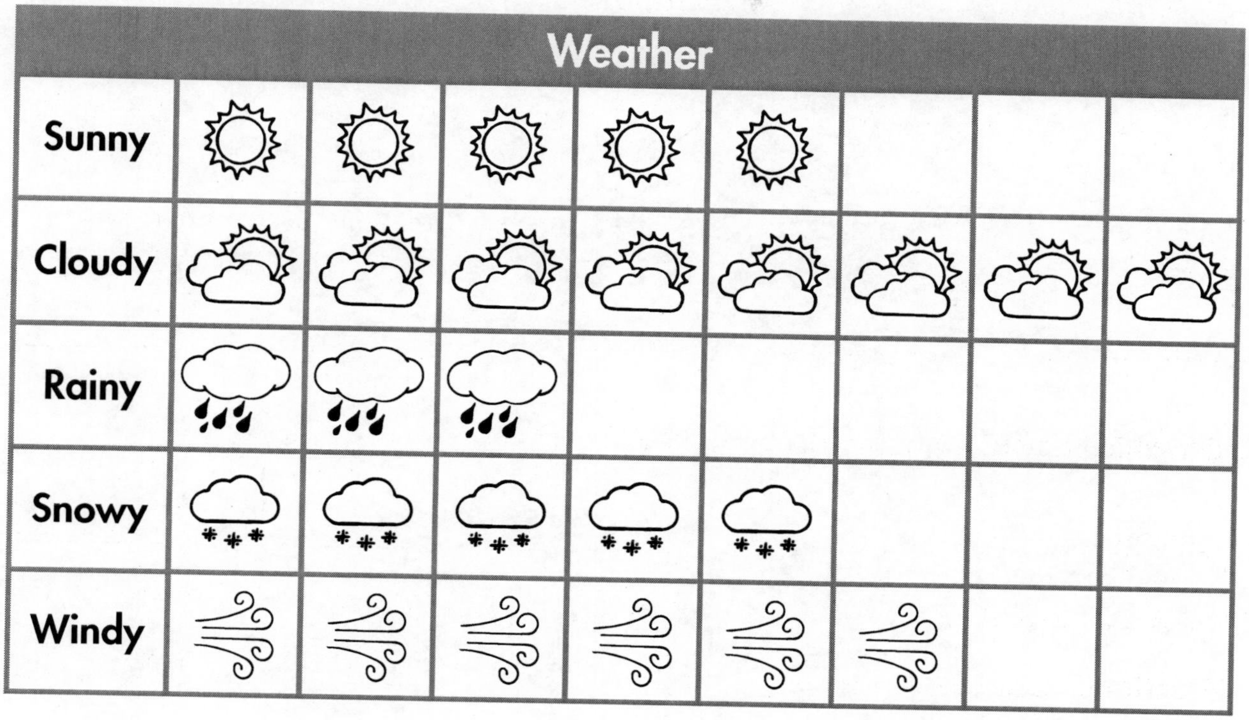

Weather								
Sunny	☼	☼	☼	☼	☼			
Cloudy	⛅	⛅	⛅	⛅	⛅	⛅	⛅	⛅
Rainy	🌧	🌧	🌧					
Snowy	❄	❄	❄	❄	❄			
Windy	🌬	🌬	🌬	🌬	🌬	🌬		

Directions: Look at the graph. Answer the questions.

1. How many days were sunny? _____

2. How many days were cloudy? _____

3. How many days were rainy? _____

4. What kind of weather happened the most? _____

5. What kind of weather happened the least? _____

Name: _____

Natural Resources

Natural means "not made by people." Rocks, trees, wind, and water are natural. We change things we get from nature into things we use:

We use plants for food.
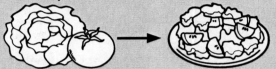

We use plants to make clothes.
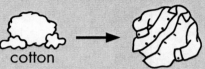
cotton

We dig rocks from the ground. We use some of them to make metal things.

We use wood from trees to build houses. We make furniture and paper, too.
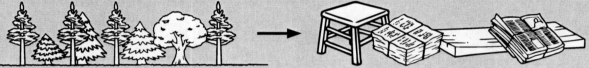

We use animals for food.
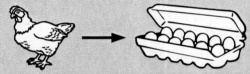

We use animals for clothing.
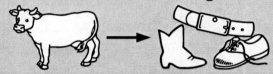

We drink water and use it to cook and clean.
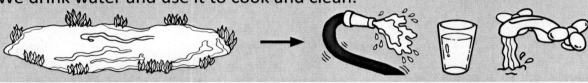

1. What does *natural* mean?
   a. something you can buy   **b.** something not made by people

2. Draw a line to match each natural resource to one way we use it.

tree   water   rocks

make a
rock wall

grow
apples

wash
dishes

Name: _____

Water

How do you get water in your home or school? Water comes out of a tap. Where does the water come from?

Water is natural. People cannot make water. We must get it from nature. We can get water from lakes and rivers. We can get it from under the ground.

First, we must clean the water. We must make it safe to drink. Then, we must send it through pipes. The pipes bring water to our buildings.

What happens to water? Where does it go when it goes down the drain? Dirty water goes down pipes. It goes to a place where it is cleaned. Some of it can be used to water plants. Some water goes into the ground. Some goes back into rivers or lakes.

1. Water is _____.
   a. a natural resource   **b.** made by people

2. After dirty water goes down the drain, it is _____.
   a. gone   **b.** cleaned

3. How do you use water? _____

_____

Name: _____

Earth Materials: Rocks, Sand, and Soil

Rocks, sand, and soil are natural. We cannot make rocks. We use rocks to make many things.

Rocks are used to make roads, walls, and buildings. Sand and soil are used to make bricks and concrete.

Special rocks are used to make metals such as steel. Steel is used to make buildings, bridges, and cars.

Sand and other crushed rocks are melted to make glass.

Most plants need soil to grow.

Some kinds of rock are made into **fuels**. A fuel is something we burn to make energy.

- We burn oil or natural gas to make our homes warm.
- We make oil into gas that makes cars and planes go.
- We use oil to make things such as plastic and crayons.

1. Can people make new rocks? **Yes** **No**

2. What is a *fuel*?

  a. a rock used to make a wall **b.** something we burn to make energy

3. Write two ways we use rocks, sand, or soil.

_____

_____

Name: _____

Living Resources

Some natural things we use are alive. Plants are alive. Animals are alive. We use plants and animals for many things.

Plants

We eat plants.

- Farmers grow fruits.
- They grow vegetables.
- They grow grains to make bread.

We use wood from trees to make things.

- We make furniture.
- We make houses.
- We make pencils.

We also use trees to make paper.

- We make books.
- We make paper bags.
- We make paper to write on.

Animals

We use things from animals.

- We drink milk from cows.
- We eat eggs from chickens.
- We use wool from sheep to make clothes.
- We need plants to feed the animals.

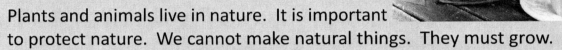

Plants and animals live in nature. It is important to protect nature. We cannot make natural things. They must grow.

1. Plants and animals are _____.
   a. natural   **b.** alive   **c.** both **a** and **b**

2. What are two ways we use plants?

   _____   _____

3. What are two ways we use animals?

   _____   _____

4. Why do we need to protect nature? _____

   _____

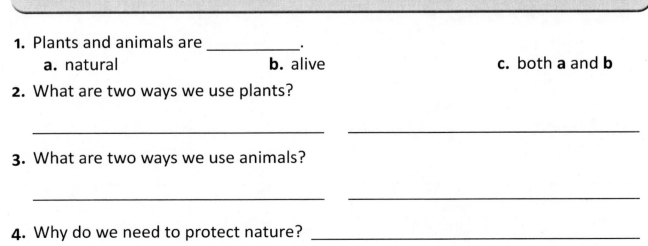

Name: _____

Conservation

We need to be careful when we use natural things. We don't want to use them up. We cannot make more natural things. We might run out of them!

When we use things, we make **waste**. *Waste* is what is left over after we use something. Trash is waste.

When we are done using things, we throw them away. We make a lot of trash. We can make less trash by not using so many things.

You can help!

- Use only the paper you need.
- Don't litter! Put all of your trash into trash cans.
- Recycle paper, glass, metal, and plastic.

Dirty water is waste. Sometimes we make the water dirty. If we are careful, we can use less water. That makes less dirty water.

You can help!

- Turn off the water while you brush your teeth.
- Take short showers.
- Don't fill the bathtub all the way.

1. Waste is _____.
   a. natural
   b. what is left over after we use something

2. What are two kinds of waste we make when we use natural things?

   _____   _____

3. What is one thing you can do to help make less waste? _____

Name: _____

Light

Have you ever been in a very dark place? Was it so dark that you couldn't see anything? Then you know that we need **light** to see things.

Light is a kind of energy. We cannot feel or hear light. We can only see it.

Light comes from a **light source**. A *light source* is anything that makes its own light. The Sun is the biggest source of light for Earth. Light bulbs are another light source we use a lot.

Light travels in rays. Light rays travel in a straight line. When light leaves a light source, the rays go in all directions.

Light rays bounce off things. When light bounces into your eyes, you can see things. If there is no light, your eyes cannot see anything.

1. We can _____ light.

   a. see   **b.** feel   **c.** hear

2. A *light source* _____.

   a. bounces light off

   b. makes its own light

3. Look around you. What light sources do you see right now?

   _____ _____

Name: _____

Light Sources

A **light source** is anything that makes its own light. There are many light sources in the world.

Natural Light

The Sun is the biggest light source for Earth. It is a **natural** light source. That means people do not make it.

The Sun shines brightly. Even at night, the Sun is still shining. We just can't see it. Our side of Earth is turned away from the Sun at night.

Other natural light sources include:

 **stars**   **lightning**   **fire**

Is the Moon a light source? It looks like it shines, but the Moon does not *make* its own light. Light from the Sun bounces off the Moon. Light from the Sun makes the Moon shine.

Man-made Light

There are light sources made by people, too. Lightbulbs use electricity to make light. Computer screens and TVs do, too!

1. Circle the light sources. Put an X on the things that are not light sources.

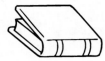   

2. Draw two light sources you have in your home or at school. Label them.

Name: _____

Light Passes Through

Light rays travel in a straight line. The rays can bounce off of things. Sometimes, they go through things.

Transparent

All or most of the light goes through some things. We call those things **transparent**. Glass windows are transparent. The light goes through them. You can see what is on the other side.

Translucent

Only some of the light goes through things that are **translucent**. When light goes through them, it looks like they are glowing. You cannot see clearly what is on the other side. Writing paper is usually translucent. Hold this paper up, and look through it toward a light. Can you see that it glows? Some of the light is coming through.

Opaque

When none of the light goes through something, we call it **opaque**. When light hits something opaque, none of it goes through. You cannot see any light or glow on the other side. Many things are opaque. Light does not go through a book or a desk.

Directions: Answer each question.

1. What do you see that lets all the light through? _____

   _____

2. What do you see that lets some of the light through? _____

   _____

3. What do you see that stops light? _____

   _____

Name: _____

Shadows

Light rays travel in a straight line until they hit something. If they cannot go through, they bounce off it.

A **shadow** is made when light cannot go through something. A *shadow* is a dark area where there is less light.

Look at the picture on the right. The light from the flashlight shines on the block. Where do you see the shadow? It is on the other side of the block. The block stops the light rays.

Look at the picture on the left. The Sun is sending out light rays. What happens when they hit the tree? They do not go through it. There is a shadow on the other side of the tree.

1. A *shadow* is _____.

   a. light rays   **b.** an area with less light

2. Look at the light sources and the objects. Draw the shadows.

Name: _____

Reflection

Light rays travel in a straight line. They keep going until they hit something. What happens then?

Light can go through some things.

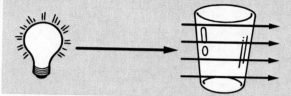

Some things **absorb** light. That means some of the light gets trapped there.

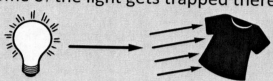

Light bounces off some things. We say that these things **reflect** light. Most things absorb some light and reflect the rest. The reflected light bounces off in all directions. That is what we see when we look at things.

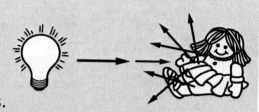

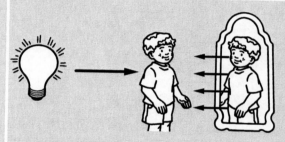

Shiny things reflect almost all the light in the same direction. Mirrors reflect light. When you look into a mirror, the light bounces straight back to your eyes. You can see yourself. You can see yourself in very still water, too.

1. When we say light gets *absorbed*, that means _____.
   a. light gets trapped
   b. light bounces off

2. What does it mean when we say light is *reflected*?
   a. light gets trapped
   b. light bounces off

3. What are two shiny things you can see yourself in? Draw them here.

Name: _____

What Is Sound?

Close your eyes. Listen carefully. What do you hear? You hear **sounds**. We cannot see sounds. We hear them with our ears.

What is sound?

➡ Sound is a kind of energy.

Where do sounds come from?

➡ Sound starts when something vibrates. **Vibrate** means "to move back and forth." Some vibrations are so fast that we can't see them. Other vibrations are much slower.

Put your fingers gently on your throat. Now, hum quietly. Can you feel the vibration?

How does sound get to us?

➡ When something vibrates, it makes the air around it vibrate, too. The vibration travels through the air. This is called a **sound wave**.

How do we hear sound?

➡ Sound waves move through the air. They reach our ears. They make a part inside our ears vibrate. Our ears send a message to our brain. Our brain makes sense of the sound.

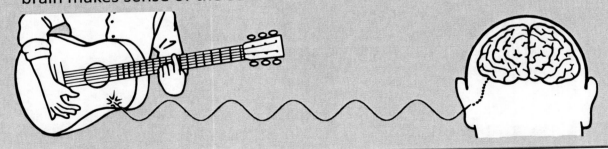

1. What does *vibrate* mean?
   a. to move back and forth   **b.** to travel through the air

2. Sound is a kind of _____.

3. What two parts of your body help you hear sounds?

_____   _____

Name: _____

How to Make Sounds

Rub your hands together. What do you hear?

You are making **vibrations**. The vibrations travel through the air. They go into your ears. Your ears send a message to your brain. That is how you hear your hands rubbing together.

Tap your fingers on your desk. What do you hear? Does it sound different from rubbing your hands together?

Here are some other ways to make sound vibrations:

Hit   **Rub**   **Shake**   **Blow**   **Sing**

Directions: Draw two things that make sound vibrations. For each one, write how you make sound with it.

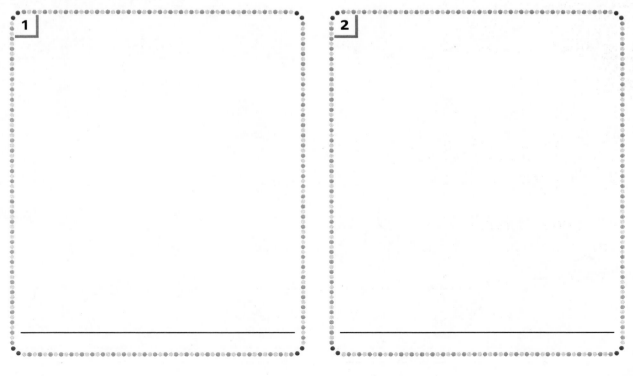

1

2

Name: _____

Sound Words

We hear many sounds every day. What sounds do you hear right now?

Sometimes, we use special words to talk about sounds. Some words *sound* like the sounds we hear.

Fireworks go **BOOM**!

The wind goes **whoosh**.

When you bite an apple, it goes **crunch**.

When a cat is happy, it **purrs**

Directions: Match each sound word to the thing that makes the sound.

| chirp | bark | tick | honk | quack | ring |

Name: _____

Loud and Quiet Sounds

Sounds have **volume**. *Volume* is how loud or quiet a sound is.

Some sounds are loud. The vibrations that make them have a lot of energy. Some sounds are so loud they hurt our ears!

Some sounds are quiet. The vibrations that make them only have a little bit of energy. Some sounds are so quiet that it is hard to hear them.

Some sounds are so quiet that we cannot hear them at all. The vibrations never reach our ears. We can't hear a butterfly's wings flapping.

1. Circle 5 things that make loud sounds. Put an X on things that make quiet sounds.

2. Draw something that makes a loud sound and something that makes a quiet sound.

Loud	Quiet

Name: _____

Musical Instruments

Do you like music? How can we make music? We can play **instruments**.
Instruments make sound vibrations.

To play some instruments, you touch the strings. You make the strings vibrate.

To play some instruments, you blow into them. The air you blow vibrates.

To play some instruments, you hit them. The flat part vibrates.

To play some instruments, you shake them. Small pieces inside vibrate.

1 Draw an instrument you hit.

2 Draw an instrument you blow into.

3 Draw an instrument you play with strings.

Name: _____

What Is Heat?

Rub your hands together really fast. What do you feel?

➡ Your hands get warmer. You feel **heat**.

➡ Heat is a kind of **energy**. We cannot see or hear heat energy. We can feel it.

Heat energy is all around you. It is in the Sun. It is in your pencil. And it is in you! Everything has heat energy.

Everything is made of tiny bits called **particles**. These small particles can move very quickly. They can bump into each other. When the particles move faster, we feel more heat.

Hot things have a lot of heat energy. Cold things have only a little heat energy. Heat moves from warmer things to cooler things.

Imagine you are standing in the sunshine. Heat from the Sun moves into your body.

When you touch an ice cube, the heat moves from your hand into the ice.

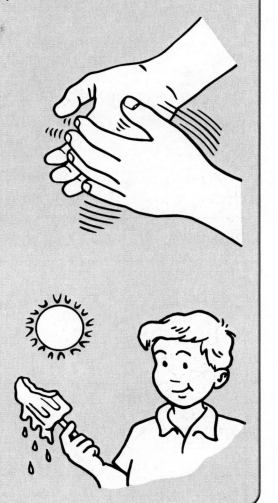

1. What is *heat*?

   a. energy we can see
   b. energy we can feel

2. You feel heat when particles move _____.

   a. faster
   b. slower

3. Heat moves from things that are warmer to things

   that are _____.

Name: _____

Heat Energy Moves

Heat energy moves. It moves from warmer things to cooler things.

There is a hot drink in this cup. The particles in the hot drink are moving quickly. They bump into the cup.

Then, the particles in the cup start to move quickly. Some of the heat energy goes from the drink to the cup.

When you touch the cup, it feels hot. That is the heat energy moving from the cup into your hand. "Heat" is just energy going into you.

Directions: Draw an arrow to show which way the heat moves.

1		2	
iron	shirt	boy	Sun
3		4	
stove	water	bread	toaster

Name: _____

Keeping Heat In

What do you do before you go outside on a cold day? You put on a jacket. Why do you do that? Because a jacket keeps you warm. How does a jacket keep you warm?

Your body has heat energy. Heat moves from warmer things to cooler things. On a cold day, heat moves from your body into the cold air. That is why you feel cold.

A jacket gets some of the heat from your body. It keeps it close to you. That is why you feel warmer with a jacket on.

This is also why a blanket keeps you warm in bed! Your body makes heat. The blanket keeps the heat close to you.

1. On a cold day, _____.

    a. heat from your body moves into the cold air.

    b. cold moves out of the air and into you.

2. Does a jacket make its own heat?

    a. Yes, a jacket makes its own heat when you wear it.

    b. No, a jacket traps heat from your body when you wear it.

3. What are some other things you wear to keep your heat in on a cold day?

_____

_____

_____

Name: _____

Heat Changes Things

Heat energy can change things.

What happens to an ice cube when it gets warm?

➡ It melts! Heat makes it change.

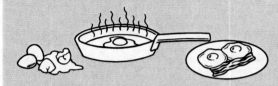 What happens to an egg when it is heated?

➡ It gets harder. We say that the egg is **cooked**. Heat makes the egg change.

What happens to wood when it is burned?

➡ It turns into ashes. Heat makes it change.

Directions: Draw how heat changes each thing.

1. **+** **=**

   ice cream   Sun

2. **+** **=**

   bread   toaster

3.  **+** **=**

   snowman   Sun

4. **+** **=**

   marshmallow   fire

Name: _____

Light, Heat, or Sound Energy?

➡ You can **see** light energy.

➡ You can **feel** heat energy.

➡ You can **hear** sound energy.

Some things put out more than one kind of energy. A fire puts out light, sound, and heat energy. You can see the light. You can hear the wood burn. You can feel the heat.

Directions: Fill in the chart. Put an X in each box to show the kind or kinds of energy each thing gives off. Some things have more than one kind of energy. **Fire** has been done for you.

		Light	Heat	Sound
1	 fire	X	X	X
2	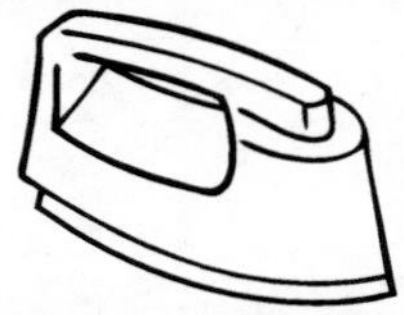 iron			
3	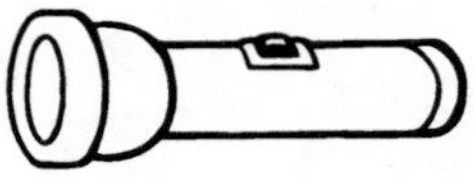 flashlight			
4	 candle			
5	 hair dryer			
6	 guitar			

Tracking Sheet

Unit 1 (pages 6–10)		Unit 8 (pages 41–45)		Unit 15 (pages 76–80)	
What Do Scientists Do?		Plants Reproduce		Four Seasons	
Observe with Tools		Seeds		Summer	
Measuring Tools		Seeds Move		Fall	
Scientists Compare Things		Match the Plant to Its Parent		Winter	
Cause and Effect		Growing a Plant		Spring	
Unit 2 (pages 11–15)		**Unit 9** (pages 46–50)		**Unit 16** (pages 81–85)	
What Are Living Things?		Animals Reproduce		Types of Weather	
What Living Things Do		Live Babies or Eggs?		Dressing for the Weather	
Living or Nonliving?		Babies That Look Like Their Parents		What Would You Do?	
Living and Nonliving Things Are Different		A Lot in Common		Read a Weather Forecast	
Living and Nonliving Parts of a Habitat		Babies That Change to Look Like Their Parents		Weather Chart	
Unit 3 (pages 16–20)		**Unit 10** (pages 51–55)		**Unit 17** (pages 86–90)	
What Living Things Need		Animals Take Care of Their Offspring		Natural Resources	
Plant Needs		Animals Prepare for Their Offspring		Water	
Animal Needs		Animals Protect Their Offspring		Earth Materials: Rocks, Sand, and Soil	
Compare a Plant and an Animal		Animals Feed Their Offspring		Living Resources	
What Am I?		Young Animals Help Themselves		Conservation	
Unit 4 (pages 21–25)		**Unit 11** (pages 56–60)		**Unit 18** (pages 91–95)	
Plants Have Roots and Stems		Animals Live in Habitats		Light	
Plants Have Leaves		Desert Habitat		Light Sources	
Plants Have Flowers		Rainforest Habitat		Light Passes Through	
Plants Have Fruits and Seeds		Polar Habitat		Shadows	
Parts of a Plant		Ocean Habitat		Reflection	
Unit 5 (pages 26–30)		**Unit 12** (pages 61–65)		**Unit 19** (pages 96–100)	
Animals and Plants Are the Same and Different		How Do You Get Energy?		What Is Sound?	
We Are the Same and Different		Animals Need Energy		How to Make Sounds	
Animals of the Same Kind		What Is a Food Chain?		Sound Words	
Animals in the Same Family		Finish the Food Chains		Loud and Quiet Sounds	
Grouping Plants		What's Missing?		Musical Instruments	
Unit 6 (pages 31–35)		**Unit 13** (pages 66–70)		**Unit 20** (pages 101–105)	
Mammals		Our Senses		What Is Heat?	
Insects		Senses Keep Us Safe		Heat Energy Moves	
Fish		Using More Than One Sense		Keeping Heat In	
Reptiles		Our Sense of Touch		Heat Changes Things	
Birds		Our Sense of Taste		Light, Heat, or Sound Energy?	
Unit 7 (pages 36–40)		**Unit 14** (pages 71–75)			
Animal Senses		Day and Night			
Animal Movement		Day and Night Skies			
Animals Eat and Drink		The Sun			
Animals Keep Warm or Cool		The Moon			
Animals Protect Themselves		Astronauts			

Answer Key

Unit 1—What Scientists Do

What Do Scientists Do? (page 6)
1. c
2. b
3. Check for appropriate answers.

Observe with Tools (page 7)
1. a
2. b
3. Circled: telescope, hand lens, and microscope
4. Check for appropriate answers.

Measuring Tools (page 8)
1. 4
2. 5
3. frog
4. 5
5. Check that container is colored to 3 liters.

Scientists Compare Things (page 9)
1. bigger
2. faster
3. Check drawings and labels for appropriate answers.

Cause and Effect (page 10)
1–3. Check for appropriate answers.

Unit 2—Living and Nonliving

What Are Living Things? (page 11)
1. Circled: kangaroo, flower, and child
2. Crossed out: spoon, glass of water, chair, and backpack

What Living Things Do (page 12)
1. grow
2. reproduce
3. learn, change

Living or Nonliving? (page 13)
1. no
2. no
3. no
4. no
5. yes
6. yes
7. yes
8. yes
9. earthworm
10. gummy worm

Living and Nonliving Things Are Different (page 14)
Check for appropriate drawings.

Living and Nonliving Parts of a Habitat (page 15)

The different shading indicates possible answers.

Living things:

trees and plants, animals, and boy

Nonliving things:

clothes, ball, house rocks, and water

Unit 3—Animals and Plants

What Living Things Need (page 16)

	Air	Food	Sunlight	Water
Plants	✓		✓	✓
Animals	✓	✓		✓

Plants make the food they need from sunlight. *Animals* benefit from sunlight, the source of all energy. Some animals need sunlight to warm their bodies. All animals need food and sunlight helps plants grow.

Plant Needs (page 17)
1.

Plants	
Need	**Do Not Need**
air Sun water	nest rock

2. Plants make their own food. They need sunlight, air, and water to make food.

Animal Needs (page 18)
Check for appropriate drawings.

Compare a Plant and an Animal (page 19)
Animal: food, shelter
Both: air, water
Plant: Sun

What Am I? (page 20)
1. both
2. animal
3. animal
4. plant
5. both

Unit 4—Parts of Plants

Plants Have Roots and Stems (page 21)
1. down
2. ground
3. water
4. Check for appropriate drawings.

Plants Have Leaves (page 22)
1. sunlight, air
2. food
3. Check for appropriate drawings.

Plants Have Flowers (page 23)
1. petals
2. Check for appropriate answers.
3. seeds
4. Check for appropriate drawings.

Plants Have Fruits and Seeds (page 24)
1. flowers
2. seeds
3. plants
4. Check for appropriate drawings.

Answer Key *(cont.)*

Parts of a Plant (page 25)
Check labels.

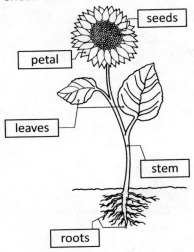

Unit 5—Animals and Plants Are the Same and Different

Animals and Plants Are the Same and Different (page 26)
1–2. Check for appropriate answers.

We Are the Same and Different (page 27)
1–4. Check for appropriate answers.

Animals of the Same Kind (page 28)
Possible answers:

Brown Bear: brown fur, eats meat, sleeps in winter
Giant Panda: black and white fur, eats only plants, stays awake in winter
Same: big, thick fur, round ears, short tails, big paws, long claws

Animals in the Same Family (page 29)
Possible answers:
1. The kittens have the same body shape and body parts. They are the same size. They have fur.
2. The kittens are different colors.

Grouping Plants (page 30)
1. cactus, rose
2. rose, strawberry (also cacti)
3. strawberry, grapes
4. lettuce, carrot

Unit 6—Animal Classes

Mammals (page 31)
1.

2. Yes. I know because I have hair and lungs and I am warm-blooded.

Insects (page 32)
1.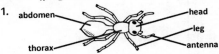
2. 6
3.
4. Students should count the legs.

Fish (page 33)
1.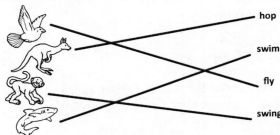
2. mammals
3. They have fins, tails, and scales.

Reptiles (page 34)
1. scales
2. Sun
3. lungs
4. land, water
5. Check for appropriate answers.

Birds (page 35)
1. feathers
2. birds
3. warm
4. eggs
5. No
6. No

Unit 7—Animal Body Parts

Animal Senses (page 36)
1. sight
2. hearing
3. smell
4. taste
5. touch

Animal Movement (page 37)

Animals Eat and Drink (page 38)
1. It cracks open fruits and seeds with its beak.
2. It holds food with its claws and eats with its sharp teeth.
3. It pulls leaves off branches with its long tongue.

Animals Keep Warm or Cool (page 39)
1. feathers
2. fur
3. wool
4. sweat
5. blubber

Animals Protect Themselves (page 40)
Check for appropriate answers.

Answer Key *(cont.)*

Unit 8—Plant Reproduction

Plants Reproduce (page 41)

1. b   2. a   3. c

Seeds (page 42)

1. c   2. seed coat   3. food

Seeds Move (page 43)

1. a
2. They fly in the wind like helicopters (spin through air).
3. (any 2) Seeds can stick to an animal's fur, get eaten by an animal, fly in the wind, float on water, pop from a pod.

Match the Plant to Its Parent (page 44)

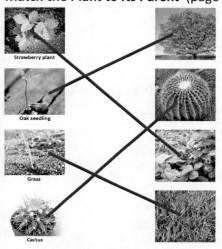

Growing a Plant (page 45)

1. c
2. Any three actions from the story in the correct order.

Unit 9—Animal Reproduction and Young

Animals Reproduce (page 46)

1. make new life
2. Check for appropriate answers/drawings.
3. Check for appropriate answers.

Live Babies or Eggs? (page 47)

1. c
2. Check for appropriate answers.
3. Check for appropriate answers.

Babies That Look Like Their Parents (page 48)

1. They have the same body shape and body parts.
2. They are different colors. The baby is smaller. The parent has a longer tail and hair.

A Lot in Common (page 49)

1–4. Check for appropriate answers.

Babies That Change to Look Like Their Parents (page 50)

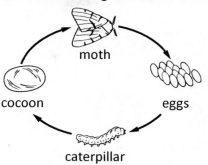

Unit 10—Animal Parent and Offspring Behaviors

Animals Take Care of Their Offspring (page 51)

1. c
2. Check for appropriate answers.
3. Check for appropriate answers.

Animals Prepare for Their Offspring (page 52)

1. c   2. a
3. She digs a den in the snow.

Animals Protect Their Offspring (page 53)

1. a
2. They work together. They chase away other animals (predators).
3. Check for appropriate answers.

Animals Feed Their Offspring (page 54)

1. b   2. c
3. One of the following:
   - They give milk to their babies.
   - They bring food to their babies.

Young Animals Help Themselves (page 55)

1. a
2.

Unit 11—Habitats

Animals Live in Habitats (page 56)

1. b   2. a
3. One of the following:
   - Their fur is the color of sand.
   - They stay in the shade during the day.
   - They get water from the plants they eat.

Answer Key *(cont.)*

Desert Habitat (page 57)
1. b
2.
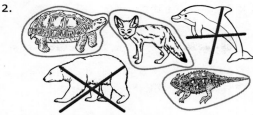

Rainforest Habitat (page 58)
1. b
2.

Polar Habitat (page 59)
1. a
2.

Ocean Habitat (page 60)
1. c
2.

Unit 12—Food Chains

How Do You Get Energy? (page 61)
1. a
2. Sun
3. Check for appropriate answers.

Animals Need Energy (page 62)
1. Sun
2. food
3. plants, meat

What Is a Food Chain? (page 63)
1. c
2.
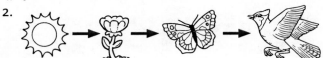

Finish the Food Chains (page 64)
1.

2.
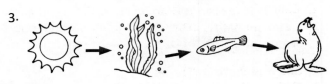

3.

4. Sun
5. frog
6. snail

What's Missing? (page 65)
1–4. Check student drawings. Discuss each chain.

Unit 13—Our Five Senses

Our Senses (page 66)
1–5. Check for appropriate answers.

Senses Keep Us Safe (page 67)
1–5. Check for appropriate answers.

Using More Than One Sense (page 68)

Which Senses Would You Use?					
	Sight	Hearing	Smell	Taste	Touch
cat	X	X			X
hot dog	X		X	X	X
xylophone	X	X			X
TV	X	X			X

Our Sense of Touch (page 69)
1. large, rough, warm, smooth, cold, small
2. Check for appropriate answers.

Answer Key (cont.)

Our Sense of Taste (page 70)

1.
   turtle candy pancakes

   book broccoli fire

2. Check for appropriate answers.
3. Check for appropriate answers.

Unit 14—Space

Day and Night (page 71)

1. B, A
2. O, X
3. △, ☐
4. ☀, ☾
5. Check for appropriate drawings.

Day and Night Skies (page 72)

Day: Sun, rainbow, lizard
Night: stars, bat, owl
Both: Moon, clouds, plane, lightning
Note: Lightning is not as easy to see during the day, but it does occur.

The Sun (page 73)

1. b
2. a
3. We need the Sun's heat to live.

The Moon (page 74)

1. b
2. b
3. We only see the part that the Sun is shining on.

Astronauts (page 75)

1. b
2. space suits
3. There is no air. It gets very hot and very cold.

Unit 15—Seasons

Four Seasons (page 76)

Season	Weather	Plants
Winter	coldest	Plants stop growing.
Spring	warmer	**Plants start growing.**
Summer	**hottest**	Plants have lots of leaves.
Fall	cooler	Leaves fall off trees.

Summer (page 77)

1. b
2. b
3. Find a lot of food or baby animals grow bigger.
4. Check for appropriate answers.

Fall (page 78)

1. a
2. b
3. Check for appropriate drawings.

Winter (page 79)

1. b
2. a
3. Some animals sleep in winter. Some animals search for food in the snow.

Spring (page 80)

1. b
2. born
3. It is warmer, and they get water from the rain.

Unit 16—Weather

Types of Weather (page 81)

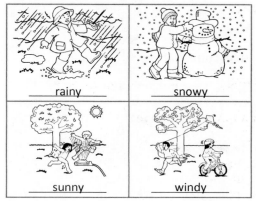

Dressing for the Weather (page 82)

What Would You Do? (page 83)

Check for appropriate drawings and explanations.

Read a Weather Forecast (page 84)

1. snowy
2. Thursday
3. Friday
4–7. Monday—cloudy, Tuesday—cloudy, Wednesday—snowy, Thursday—rainy, Friday—windy

Answer Key *(cont.)*

Weather Chart (page 85)

1. 5 days   3. 3 days   5. rainy
2. 8 days   4. cloudy

Unit 17—Earth's Environment

Natural Resources (page 86)

1. b
2.

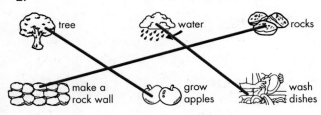

Water (page 87)

1. a   2. b
3. Check for appropriate answers.

Earth Materials: Rocks, Sand, and Soil (page 88)

1. No   2. b
3. Check for appropriate answers.

Living Resources (page 89)

1. c
2. Check for appropriate answers.
3. Check for appropriate answers.
4. We need to protect nature because we cannot make natural things.

Conservation (page 90)

1. b
2. trash and dirty water
3. Check for appropriate answers.

Unit 18—Light Energy

Light (page 91)

1. a   2. b
3. Check for appropriate answers.

Light Sources (page 92)

1.

2. Check for appropriate drawings and labels.

Light Passes Through (page 93)

1–3. Check for appropriate answers.

Shadows (page 94)

1. b
2. Check for appropriate drawings.

Reflection (page 95)

1. a   2. b
3. Check for appropriate drawings.

Unit 19—Sound Energy

What Is Sound? (page 96)

1. a   2. energy   3. ears, brain

How to Make Sounds (page 97)

1–2. Check for appropriate drawings and answers.

Sound Words (page 98)

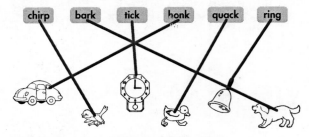

Loud and Quiet Sounds (page 99)

1.

2. Check for appropriate drawings.

Musical Instruments (page 100)

1–3. Check for appropriate drawings.

Unit 20—Heat Energy

What Is Heat? (page 101)

1. b   2. a   3. cooler

Heat Energy Moves (page 102)

1. iron → shirt   3. stove → water
2. boy ← Sun   4. bread ← toaster

Keeping Heat In (page 103)

1. a   2. b
3. Check for appropriate answers.

Heat Changes Things (page 104)

1. melted ice cream
2. toast
3. melted snowman
4. toasted marshmallow

Light, Heat, or Sound Energy? (page 105)

2. heat (sometimes sound)
3. light (sometimes heat)
4. light, heat
5. sound, heat
6. sound